Push Yourself!

Self-Motivation for Christian Workers

Abb Thomas

Acknowledgment-Dedication

I met Kerby Richmon near the swamps of Louisiana, where I tasted my first alligator meal. In later years, we sought a man to replace me in a much larger church setting with the children here in Milford. Kerby would be that man.

After directing our Sunday school and children's ministry, we again sought a man to replace me and to direct Master Ministries, which is the umbrella name for all of our ministries, including the largest, Master Club. This is a children's ministry for three-year-olds through grade six. The clubs are in over 600 churches today and growing! See the work at masterclubs.org.

With great joy, Kerby Richmon replaced me again! He has the passion, the high-level commitment, the love for God and His church, the technical skills of this new age, and the wisdom to lead us into greater years than we have ever seen!

Kerby, may the glory of God continue to be your goal and may God's richest blessings be upon you and your wife, Virginia. May God answer your greatest prayers and may your prayers be larger than ever.

My wife and I love you and your family.

Contents

Introduction

*W*hy self-motivation? I have now had forty-two years of ministry in two large churches, both with aggressive pastors. Both believe that the Great Commission is given by God to the church to be fulfilled by those who serve the Lord. The lack of motivation is so often missing from both leadership and those that follow.

The work of God is completed by those who spend their time on the details. Most workers will never preach a sermon publicly, but will still administrate the church of God. It's where the details make the difference.

Set your goals higher, hang up your signs with greater numbers, but someone had better be found *striving* toward those goals.

The greatest pastor ever can still not do it all. The pastor who will not release leadership to others will soon find his personal level of incompetence. We all do.

All through scriptures, we see Paul and others who trained workers and then sent them forth. In our churches today, it's now our turn to lead. We must continue to train our church servants or we are in for a long, slow growth process, and in many cases, the Great Commission is literally ignored.

However, it should not be so, and it doesn't have to be so. Someone in your ministry needs to lead the charge with both spiritual vision of the job at hand and the motivation of those servants who will get the work accomplished.

The church of God needs the vision of God, which comes from the Word of God. The pastor casts the vision to the church body. When the vision has great *clarity*, every believer understands his personal role and growth and salvation will increase.

Most workers in a church need more motivation than they have now. Self-motivation often has to be taught to many workers. This book is prepared to help *push* key leaders who will again *push* others.

Within the contents listing, you will see the areas we intend to develop. Our overriding theme on each and almost every page is to *push yourself* to be more than you are today for the glory of God tomorrow.

I have spent my years not as a pastor but always down where the details made the difference. My goal has long been to complement my pastor. He needs everyone he can get "down in the pits," as I have often called it. It's down where the details will make the difference in any endeavor.

It often takes weeks and months for the magnificent to happen in ministry. It happens *because* several have taken care of the details.

God has called the pastor to especially be "God-ward," as Moses was counseled to be by his father-in-law, Jethro: "Hearken now unto my voice, I will give thee counsel, and God shall be with thee: Be thou for the people God-ward, that thou mayest bring the causes unto God" (Exodus 18:19). Your pastor must have the time for study, prayer, counsel, and finding the mind of God on all church matters. He cannot be at his best unless the servants of God are self-motivated and striving for the vision that he has already cast for the church.

Therefore, you, as a reader of this book, could take the principles within and lead the group of servants at your church. The *details* will make the difference.

1

Effort Proves The Stuff
You Are Made Of!

Preview...

Effort Proves the Stuff You are Made of!

You had better believe that *effort* will get you to meet goals you have set or the lack of effort will bring failure far too often.

"*Effort* before fame" is what brought the successes we have read about.

Effort is everything. Vince Lombardi, (who led the Green Bay Packers football team to five NFL championships and won the first two Super Bowls) said: "Winning is not everything—but making the *effort* to win is."

The effort to out-achieve yourself brings great gain. It takes effort to concentrate and focus.

The overriding theme throughout this book is to "push yourself." It's the same thing, the act of effort. Effort establishes the habit of self-discipline.

Effort—The Ultimate Measure of Success

*I*n John Wooden's book *Wooden on Leadership*, he says, "There is a standard higher than merely running the race. Effort is the ultimate measure of your success." That is a powerful statement.

Wooden's legendary UCLA run of ten NCAA national basketball championships in twelve years included eighty-eight consecutive winning games and four perfect seasons. Yet, his leadership of students and young men peaked higher than wins on a basketball court. He instilled winning for all of life in everyone he touched. He attributes *effort* as the ultimate measure of success.

Dad loved effort. When he told me to "git er' done, boy," he was talking about effort. He worked hard for his family on the Southern Railroad. He put effort in for his family in the Great Depression. Looking back now, I see far more effort and sacrifice by my parents than I understood as a child. Dad taught me how to hunt and fish, which was a large part of our diet in those days. He also taught me to do things well in order to see good results. I was taught to walk silently through the woods, to whisper, to avoid making the noises that scattered the game. Those were good days and good beginnings. Even hunting and fishing are enhanced by effort!

Personal Effort Brings Personal Gain!

The effort it takes to concentrate and focus on the needs at hand develops character for all of life to follow. We can all see and respect others who excel in their chosen fields. Effort before fame is what brought them to that level of recognition. We recognize effort as we experience fulfillment in the project at hand. On the inside, we know whether that effort was our best or less than our best. The applause we may receive lasts for the moment, but the satisfaction comes from the intrinsic feelings of fulfillment. That feeling never comes when the effort has been shallow. We know, based on our inherent feelings of approval or disapproval, how much effort we gave.

Our lives can be humble and low key to the public, yet satisfying and fulfilling within because of effort. Some are fortunate enough to amass great fortunes and notoriety, while others are seen only by their families or in their small town. Effort is not measured by the front-page articles, but by that self-awareness of giving all we have! A great example of effort is drawn from comments by the twenty-sixth president of the United States, Theodore Roosevelt, when he said:

"The credit belongs to the man who is actually in the arena; whose face is marred by the dust and sweat and blood; who strives valiantly; who errs and comes short again and again; who knows the great enthusiasm, the great devotions, and spends himself in a worthy cause; who at the best knows in the end that triumph of high achievement; and who at the worst if he fails, at least fails while daring greatly."

Winning Is Not Everything—Effort Is!

Vince Lombardi led the green Bay Packers to five NFL Championships and won the first two Super Bowls. He said: "I firmly believe that any man's finest hour—his greatest fulfillment to all he holds dear—is that moment when he has worked his heart out in a good cause and lies exhausted on the field of battle—victorious."

Effort! Effort! Lombardi also said: "Winning is not everything—but making the effort to win is."

Golda Meir was the fourth prime minister of the State of Israel, beginning in 1969. "Her true strength and spirit were emphasized when, after her death in 1978, it was revealed that she had suffered from leukemia for twelve years" From *"Great Quotes from Great Leaders"*,compiled by Peggy Anderson.

Andrew Carnegie came to America from Scotland in 1848. Through steady effort, he invested wisely to amass high wealth. One of his efforts was to create thousands of public libraries over the world. He said this as we think about effort: "The average person puts only 25% of his energy and ability into his work. The world takes off its hat to those who put in more than 50% of their capacity, and stands on its head for those few and far between souls who devote 100%."

Effort to Out-Achieve Yourself Brings Great Gain!

From the Christian perspective we know that someday we stand before the Lord, who is not only our Savior but our ultimate judge. The effort we have given to serve Him may not be known to the public, but it is recorded by our dear Lord.

He knows my effort exerted amid the problems, delays, temptations, the wiles of the devil, and the efforts of those nominal

"Christians" that always come short of faith. I must give effort that pleases the Lord. That effort is known and remembered by the dear Lord. The day and time to serve the Lord is now. The effort to be extended is now!

Many weeks I am facing the leaders of church classes, always along with some school teachers in our four-hour sessions around the country. Part of my effort is to move them to greater effort. To out-achieve themselves as teachers is what everyone I have ever seen in forty years needs. I have only met two who claimed to have "arrived." But in two minutes of conversation, you arrive at the opposite conclusion.

Effort Covers Us All!

Most teachers could stand to read a lot more books, try more techniques, listen to tapes, and attend training seminars. The effort to schedule such during their weeks ahead will bring great gain!

It actually begins with me. I must put in the effort myself in order to help them. One way I do this is to select the twenty best books I have read on teaching and reread each this coming year, along with anything new I can find.

Business books give you the best principles from those who excel. For the teachers, I try to enhance their year with a truth from a book they would never select to read. But the truth of that business book could revolutionize their teaching in the classroom. The best book we publish is titled *Teaching!* It includes quotes from fifty other authors. I had to read all those books to find the help I could pass on to other teachers who never read. Yes, it takes extra effort, but I want to be that kind of help.

I cherish what I call book review notes that I keep in binders. Once a good book is read and underlined, I then take those key thoughts, great quotes, and one-liners and type them up in four to six page summaries. When in the van or motel or sitting in a doctor's office, waiting for who knows how long, I can then take ten minutes to read the very best lines from that good book. Once again, I feed my mind with those good thoughts. I want to push myself.

It Takes Effort to Concentrate and Focus

In all probability, these two are hard for you too—to *concentrate* and *focus* all you have on the task at hand. But, when you do, you win! Whatever the circumstances, creating the ideal environment for concentration and focus is your goal. It may be different for you than for me.

My ideal place to concentrate would be in a cabin atop a mountain in the Smokies. But, in reality, I would probably just sit and look at the scenery much of the day or take a hike, find a quiet stream, look for wildlife, enjoy a waterfall, or take pictures. My reason for going to the perfect place could easily change by the time I got there. It sounds good, but if I can't concentrate and focus here, I probably won't there either.

To concentrate, I will need to remind myself of the great benefit it brings and of the personal achievement these two words will add to my own value. If I'm bad at it, how will I teach others to be good at it?

It Takes Effort to Push Yourself

The overriding theme throughout this book is to *push yourself.* It's the same thing, the act of effort.

In the excellent book *The Laws of Lifetime Growth*, by Dan Sullivan and Catherine Nomura, one chapter is titled "Always Make Your Performance Greater Than Your Applause." Here is a quote from this chapter: "Continually work to surpass everything you've done so far, and your performance will always be greater than your applause." They continue:

"You have control over your performance. You never have control over other people's response, approval, or applause. The goal here is always to be getting better; to appreciate how far you've come, but also to keep striving to go further, always making your future bigger than your past . . . a bigger future requires that your skill and mastery keep improving."

Words like those confirm the great value of the effort we give. Without that continual effort, dreams fade, the past abilities grow old, and our value to others fades.

Effort becomes your time, your money, your sacrifice, and your total thought brought to a point of achievement.

Effort, when it begins to wane, cries out to your will for assistance. Your will agrees with your original motives for starting the project. Bring them up again. Say them to yourself out loud. Ask God to rekindle the fire, and efforts will stand you on your feet again.

Effort identifies you from the inside out. It's that constant drive, that push, that tenacity within. It is not up today, gone tomorrow; it becomes a habit throughout life. The external factors that frequent our course must be kept in check by the effort we make to keep the anchor out of the water at all times.

Always push yourself through your effort to keep the next step in sight. The affairs of life may cause the end of the distant rainbow to fade for short periods of time, but the next step is still within full view. Effort can get you to the next step, which clears the fog to the next one. It's that effort, that value of life that keeps you moving!

Effort Brings Creative Thoughts

Read, *think*, and *apply* are words that solve a lot of problems for anyone on the move. Chapter 15, "Reading Inspires Me, Motivates Me, and Pushes Me," will help you to see that effort is tied to all three.

Reading educates me so that my efforts are not in vain.
Thinking helps me cross bridges before I get there.
I *apply* the effort to put all the pieces together.

Creativity brings with it a patient effort. Time in association, brainstorming, listening to options, and evaluating the outside-the-box ideas takes up valuable time. But it is time well spent. Options solve problems. Options bring better ways, before unknown. Creativity is mostly innovation. That takes time to think it through.

Creative thought solves problems, stretches possibilities, and expands solutions. Pick up and go with it!

Effort—Establishes the Habit of Self-Discipline

Self-discipline is one of those subjects that we all hear about and cheer about. But when the seminar is over, so is all the motivation.

Self-discipline sounds like it hurts, but like push-ups and the treadmill, it eventually shows great gain. Effort will get you to this great practice of self-discipline faster than you think.

We must come to reality, to understand that my ship may have sunk instead of being about to arrive. My rich uncle needs more of my help than I can get from him. The lottery takes, not gives; perhaps you didn't know that? Tomorrow is not your lucky day.

Therefore, plan effort for tomorrow. Remember, you haven't yet made any mistakes tomorrow. Look up, bring on the effort, and let it be the stuff you are made of!

Effort Is a Day by Day Thing!

Your routine of day to day achievement will benefit your life from now on!

Larry Winget gave advice to graduates of 2012, as seen on Fox News, May 15, 2012: "If you don't know how to be worth more than you cost, then employers will pass you over and find someone else." In other words, your *effort* will keep the first and the last job you ever have.

Then he said: "Some people work hard yet are not any good at what they do, so it doesn't matter. And I know people who are excellent at what they do, but they didn't work hard enough at it to make any difference."

Effort will always be a huge plus in our life. It will bring more personal fulfillment, more worth in the workplace, and be pleasing to God.

Perhaps you remember the outstanding Bible story found in Nehemiah as he challenges his countrymen to arise and rebuild the destroyed walls of Jerusalem. "So built we the wall; and all the wall was joined together unto the half thereof: for the people had a mind to work" (Nehemiah 4:6).

Football was a good place for effort to be on display. In practice sessions, effort often put you on the first team or on the bench. One of our big wiry-tough tacklers insisted on everyone putting as much effort into practice as he did. When he spotted an underachiever in effort, he asked coach to line him up on the tackle practice sessions. Coach always complied. When their time came to butt heads, he would make their teeth chatter, and flinching or avoiding the contact only brought a heavier pounding. He cured a lot of our effortless players.

Effort will always be a part of pushing yourself. You never grow out of the need for effort you can now give physically, but effort still comes from within.

So, where am I today? Do I give the effort that leaves me comforted on the inside that I gave it my all, my full 100 percent? Do you want a life of self-discipline? Effort will keep it going when the body is not so excited about it.

Let's end our thoughts as we began, with the quote by John Wooden: "There is a standard higher than merely running the race. *Effort* is the ultimate measure of your success."

Key Thoughts to Remember/Action Tips

1. Try this: On a small card, small enough to carry in your pocket or purse, print in large letters the word EFFORT! As you go through the week you will see or feel the card as a reminder, maybe twenty times this week, that EFFORT! is your goal. This is how you develop the habit of reminding yourself to put effort into your work. We all want it, but without a habitual reminder it may never be a way of life. The card system has been such a help to me, having used many words like that to develop the habit and to get it up and running in my life!

2. List points of effort for each major project this week.

3. Memorize John Wooden's great statement and quote it at the beginning of every day: "There is a standard higher than merely running the race. *Effort* is the ultimate measure of your success."

2

Fulfillment Keeps The Dreams Alive!

Preview...

The dictionary defines it this way: 1) To carry out something promised. Cause to be or happen. 2) To do something required. 3) To bring to an end, complete. 4) To realize completely one's ambitions, potentialities.

So fulfillment is felt within when a goal is accomplished. Smaller feelings of fulfillment happen more often as steps to the goal are accomplished, each bringing us closer to completion. Each fulfillment energizes enough effort to take the next step! Satisfaction within moves us to want more.

Fulfillment drives you to *push yourself!* Fulfillment makes you constantly thirsty for more. The dreams within you are at stake. The satisfaction does not lull you to sleep, but rather it awakens you to the desire for more. It's an adrenaline push. Fulfillment gets the encouragement level to a new high.

---

*F*ulfillment. There's *your push!*
The fulfillment of a job well done is welcome to one isolated individual, to small and large groups, to companies, and even to nations. Like the God-given senses that cross all cultural boundar-

ies, fulfillment is a built-in encourager for people worldwide. The absence of a goal worth pursuing has led people to bum status and even to suicide. For whatever the reason, joy has left the building. Initiative is hard to muster. Self-pity, or the lowest of self-esteem, is on the throne now. There's no light at the end of the tunnel when fulfillment is lacking.

The goal is to learn to *push myself* before the negative occurs. I can watch for the symptoms and then take very quick steps of realignment. Fulfillment is obviously healthier than being in lack of a daily purpose.

Seeing the milestone markers pass by should bring fulfillment. Stopping to review, evaluate, and relive the victories of the past returns the fulfillment. Past dreams should not be the end of our fulfillment, but encouragement to see some more. Past dreams should *push you*, not retire you.

One success moves us toward another. In my years with Dr. Lee Roberson, every day was "something day" at our church. Why? Because a new goal moves you to work at it rather than having no goal at all. Every class, every department, every person was heading for a goal every week. That was back when few churches were mega-sized as today. This church was second- and then third-largest in the nation. The motivation got us all working, and the goal reached brought fulfillment! From my early thirties to the early seventies, the desire for that feeling of fulfillment is still there! That *pushes me!*

> *He will fulfill the desire of them that fear him:*
> *he also will hear their cry, and will save them.*
> —Psalm 145:19

Fulfillment is what we were made for. We read of multiple symptoms and physical illnesses that come from depression. I believe the lack of personal fulfillment could be traced back to the feelings and sicknesses of many.

Talk about symptoms, my doctor just laid a big one on me. I needed more help in understanding my sickness. It wasn't funny at the time, but it is now. My doctor gave me his diagnosis on one of my visits. When he finished, I could only stare at him. I had nothing to say. I understood a whole lot of nothing. I still didn't know what I had. So, in my own brand of ignorance I asked the doctor to write it out for me. Here goes:

"You have a type II acromion with mild to moderate down slope. The cuff is diffusely hypertrophic and tendinopathic a moderate to very severe peritendinopathic, the result being outlet-related cuff impingement. Furthermore, interstitial degeneration without focal fluid defect to suggest a partial or full-thickness tear."

I had that. In common terms that I could understand, all of that meant that my arm hurt really bad. I looked on the back side of the sheet he gave me to see a list of 236 diagnoses that could be made from your waist to your neck. And that did not include things like the heart, lungs, liver, or other major organ.

The emptiness of evolution has to be a depressing thought. Because of my faith in Christ, I can't feel those feelings. But having talked to many over the years who believe there is no God, no Creator-Designer, the answers to the fulfillment questions are just not there. Why am I here? What is my daily purpose? What is my ultimate end? Try finding fulfillment in being the next step above the apes. I've often wondered if we evolved from the apes; why do we still have apes that have never evolved? Try finding fulfillment in random chance, to live, to die, and then to simply poof away to nowhere for evermore. How depressing. Where's the fulfillment in life?

But we can look the other way and be an achiever of dreams! See yourself with greater goals, greater ambitions, and plenty of room for more fulfillment, regardless of age. How exciting it is to see elderly folks who have yet to give up and with no intentions to do so. Shuffleboard is not fulfilling enough for them. They have learned to *push themselves!*

Once you've had that good taste of fulfillment, you want it again. Fulfillment fills! It is what's well worth the conscious effort to *push yourself* for more.

Many who have honed their skills for forty years in a career or trade find it extremely hard to live a life of leisure. It may be a novelty for six months or so, but often the itch comes back. Something is missing in life, and I believe often that the feeling of fulfillment is not there anymore. The honey-do lists have all been done, and there is little on the list for the next day.

We are seeing more missionaries go to the fields of the world at later ages than ever before. They have had their careers (fulfilling) but now at fifty-five, sixty, sixty-five years of age they just don't want to stop. Their skills are at their highest level. Experience has weeded out most of the youthful mistakes. Why not spend the rest of your life active, alive, energetic, and fulfilled? It's a big question, and once you answer it, there's *your push!*

Bobby Bowden coached for many years at Florida State University. When he was eighty, some were calling for him to resign as head coach. In a virtual tie in the records for most wins in a major college football program, controversy gained momentum as their year seemed to be heading for a losing season.

Coach Bowden responded, "At age sixty I thought of retiring at sixty-five. When sixty-five came, I still felt good. We were still winning, and so seventy didn't seem so far off. At seventy, and still feeling good, seventy-five didn't sound so bad either. Now, approaching eighty, that doesn't sound bad either." In other words, if the capability, dream, and passion are still there, why give up the fulfillment in life?

It's a fair question. If you can still physically, mentally, and motivationally continue that passionate dream, why stop? Many coaches have gone down fast after that daily purpose was taken away.

What is fulfillment for you? Whatever it is for you, it will not arrive without your striving toward that goal. It will probably require some mastery on your part, but even finding mastery brings fulfillment!

For example, if you are a teacher, fulfillment doesn't come by preparing just enough to get by next week. Eventually, guilt will come instead of that wonderful feeling of fulfillment.

Your preparation—studying, planning, preparing—will make your presentation fulfilling. The lack or slack in preparation brings less than fulfillment. Oh, others may compliment you on a good lesson or good class, but you know deep down inside it was nowhere near your best. Your best takes effort, and fulfillment doesn't come from less than your best. The joy of striving and mastering brings the greatest feeling of all!

I have met so many over the years who give the same account, "I went to college for a year or two or even three, but never finished." Everyone, without exception, quickly follows by saying, "But I wish to this day that I had finished my goal." For some that was forty years ago, and they're still wishing things had turned out differently. It's still gnawing at them.

In my teacher training sessions, I have yet to put it all on DVDs. I have been asked to often, and perhaps I will. But for me, it's all been wrapped up in that feeling of fulfillment. I have always traveled to each training site for a reason. I want to bring all the books, teaching aids, posters, and visuals with me so teachers can see. I lug boxes of books they can buy. The PowerPoint presentation is a necessity. I carry my own large screen, computer, and projector just to make sure it's right. It takes me four hours to set up the auditorium. But, most of all I prefer a live session so I can put some feeling, emotion, expression, and loads of passion in what I have to say. I want them to feel, hear, and see just how significant the principles of teaching really are.

One of my visuals is a very bright thermometer called "The Teacher Significance O'Meter." Every few pages, the thermometer gives a loud "Whoosh" and goes up another notch. It reinforces their significance in the classroom.

For me, the whole plan is what brings fulfillment. I'm sure the day is coming when all of that is too much for me to handle, and I dread it. That's when I'm at my best. That's fulfillment. That's what has driven me to keep on *pushing myself!* Every week, just before the session begins, I'm in a back room somewhere doing my self-talk. I'm trying to *push myself!* It's a reminder again of the purpose of teacher training. It's why I'm here. They need what they're about to get. It will help them greatly. I can't wait! By the time the introduction is finished by a pastor, I'm about to explode. If he goes a bit too long, I walk closer as if to say, "Let's move!"

For you, whatever the career, you know there's a best level of performance, and there's a less than your best. What's it going to be? *Push yourself!*

Key Thoughts to Remember/Action Tips

1. Share your fulfillment with your spouse—always.
2. List here to remind yourself of the three highest reasons for your dream:

   a. _____

   _____

   b. _____

   _____

   c. _____

   _____

3. Celebrate again the steps already attained toward your dream.
4. Begin each day with a positive reading of your goal, your daily purpose, that which brings you the personal joy deep down inside.
5. At week's end, list your victories and rejoice.
6. Questions to ask yourself in all honesty:

   a. _____
   Do I know exactly what I want?

   b. _____

   c. _____
   Can I list the price I will need to pay to achieve it?

   d. _____
   Am I busy paying my part of the price?

   e. _____
   If not, why not? If not, when do I begin?

7. _____
   Schedule a time for facing the facts, asking yourself those hard questions, and coming up with an answer.
8. _____
   Fulfillment does not arrive unexpectedly. When I anticipate victory, it is because I have worked toward it!

3

Out-Achieving Myself
Is The Best Comparison!

Preview...

Achievement brings fulfillment! The more I can be a part of an achievement goal, the more fulfillment comes. We are dealing here with my own personal fulfillment. It's what I'm feeling inside.

Therefore, as an individual, if I can out-achieve my personal best, the fulfillment keeps rising. If I always compare my accomplishments with someone else, I may beat myself up rather than encourage myself. This swings the pendulum the other way, and past momentum is lost again.

I must concentrate on out-achieving myself!

*W*hat is possible for you to achieve? Exclude all the *buts*, *ifs*, *probably can'ts*, and all of your *maybes*. Without the preconceived thoughts of what you could never achieve, but with the thought of reaching your highest dream, what would that dream be? Don't even compare your big dream with someone else's big dream. Their finances, experiences, work force, and the like may be far above where you are at present. Just make your big dream big for you!

As you think, so you go—and so goes your career and mission in life.

At a local town fair, Elsie Toots came out the winner of the chocolate-eating contest for the seventh year. Elsie was given the Consolidated Chocolate Makers of America award as Sweetheart of the Year. She finished off twelve large boxes of chocolates. It took six men to wheel her off the platform, but the whole town had a proud moment! *(A slight joke!)*

Perhaps your goal is not as unique as someone else's, but to you it's a big-time role to play and a goal to reach. I believe the greater motivation is not another person or another competitor, but rather it lies within yourself. If I can see myself growing in knowledge, wisdom, and understanding and my skills are sharper than ever before, then out-achieving myself is the better comparison. The circumstances, personnel, or finances may not be an accurate picture with which to compare yourself to your goal in giving the best that you can produce. You always know when you are giving your best or using your abilities to their highest potential.

I love to reminisce about my ten years in Jupiter, Florida, just north of Palm Beach. It didn't take long to fall in love with skin diving. We call it *free diving*, for there are no tanks and no line guns.

We had diving teams that competed for the state championship. On our team was a guy who could hit 100 feet deep and stay there long enough to spear a fish, pull it out of a cave, and make it back to the top! I knew immediately that he was far above my ability. He was a natural. For me, it meant running in the soft sand on the beach, lifting weights, eating right, and more pure torture. It didn't take that for him, but for me it did. I had to compete against myself. There was my *push!* I started out going to the depth of 30 feet, then 40 feet, and then 50 feet. After another year, I could hit 60 feet. I was learning to *push myself!* Another two years of experience and I could hit 70 feet, and that became my practical limit.

In sports especially, there's always someone down the road who can beat you at your best. But what is *your* best? That's what counts! John Wooden during his years of ten national college basketball championships, said it like this in the book *"Wooden On Leadership"*:

27

"Success is always attainable when defined correctly. That is, as making the effort to do the best of which you are capable. With that as your standard you will not fail. Competitive greatness is not defined by victory nor denied by defeat. It exists in the effort that precedes those two "impostors" as well as their accomplices: fame, fortune, and power. Measurements of success I rejected long ago."

And again he said, "There is a standard higher than merely winning the race: *Effort* is the ultimate measure of your success."

Winston Churchill influenced his country to stand against the wickedness of Hitler's Germany. England had not been this way before. He added his influence to that of Franklin D. Roosevelt and Joseph Stalin to determine the strategy for World War II. He *pushed himself* to be a courageous leader and to push his country to stand bravely. He had become more than he was for such a challenge. We still talk about him seventy years later!

Martin Luther King Jr. had little to compare himself with. Instead, he rose to the occasion and influenced a successful boycott of the segregated system in Montgomery, Alabama, in 1955. His influence began to remove the humiliating treatment of black Americans. I can remember those days and the "White Only" signs here and there. He out-achieved himself. His influence for rights through peaceful protests will continue his influence throughout our lifetimes.

It would be a great thing to consider the areas where you can out-achieve yourself. Try one or two of your significant areas to start. Brainstorm a series of questions, forcing yourself to come up with the answer. What was my original purpose? Is this still intact? If not, why not? How is my efficiency? How is my overall achievement? How is my time management? Can I out-achieve my goals of last year? Can I read five books more than last year? Could I achieve a higher level of giving to worthwhile causes? Can I help a struggling college student?

Out-achieving myself gives great rewards. Can I out-achieve my expressions of love for my wife than I gave last year? Can I put a note in my pocket with only one or two words that will remind me each day to work toward that goal? *Push yourself!*

In *Monday Morning Choices*, David Cottrell says, "Without fail, when you embrace this 'why me' attitude, the victim mentality will paralyze your attitude and your enthusiasm."

The blame game is not good. When you own the set goal, you then own the victories or the losses. But that's fine, for no one is perfect anyway. You will ultimately be the one to decide if you will have the attitude of an achiever or a loser. You must be in control of your choices.

In fact, your attitude will be a major part of out-achieving yourself. Without the proper attitude or outlook, achieving goals will be rare in your life. The push will not be there to help you to out-achieve yourself.

Attitudes give testimony to the deep-down beliefs you hold. Without this strong passionate push from within, the drive to excel will not be enough. The drive within supersedes any pep talk the boss can give or any self-talk I can do for myself.

In the Christian world, our key word is *faith*. Faith is above and beyond my ability to accomplish within myself or by my own resources. If I have the ability to accomplish the task, then do it. If I need it and have the resources for it, then go ahead and get it. I don't need faith for what I can see, but I do for what I cannot see.

Faith comes in when it's above and beyond my ability. So, what's on my list that I must trust God for? Faith trusts the Lord to bring it to pass, as I trust Him for it. Thus, I can trust God to actually do far and above that which I could ever do. Again, it all comes from deep down inside, from the hearts of men and women.

> *It is difficult if not impossible to be remarkable at*
> *doing something you don't have your heart in.*
> —Mark Sanborn, *Encore Effect*

We, therefore, can do above and beyond our highest dreams to date. With that attitude, we are willing to tackle that giant-sized dream! We can out-achieve any project done thus far. It can be above our abilities and above our resources, and yet we can out-achieve anything we have ever attempted!

If it takes a newly developed skill, I can develop that skill. There's *my push!*

Again, in the book *Monday Morning Choices,* we read, "The choice of persistence is about setting a goal and reaching it, about coming to roadblocks and hurdling them, about continuing the journey in spite of life's speed bumps." What an excellent thought! I don't want to go through life without the desire to accomplish more than I have already accomplished. I can't live on yesterday's goals and accomplishments. That time of fulfillment lasted for the moment, but the moment is long gone.

> *No one plans to become mediocre. Rather,*
> *mediocrity is the result of no plan at all.*
> —Tom Newberry, *Success Is Not an Accident*

It seems so logical to be able to out-achieve yourself. Take your last big task completed. Now, consider this: (1) I have seen and measured the results of my last big accomplishment. (2) I have in mind the mistakes made last time. With evaluation and thought I could do it again without those mistakes! (3) I could probably see ways to do it cheaper next time. (4) With brainstorming for new ideas, my coworkers could help me to see an even better approach. (5) Now I have increased my wisdom, knowledge, and understanding of such a project.

Could I not expect to out-achieve myself next time? Sure, unless my attitude had already taken me down failure lane and I'm ready to quit. This world is oversaturated with quitters and underachievers. Let every project and every experience *push you* to the next accomplishment!

Key Thoughts to Remember/Action Tips

1. Learn to do some self-talks. Compare a similar past project with your current project to determine to out-achieve yourself.
2. Make a short list of projects in which you could out-achieve yourself.
3. List three goals from last year, in which you could do better this year.
4. What new skills could you master this year?
5. Never fear facing these hard questions. They make you *think*, and thinking is where innovation comes from. Raise your last accomplishment to a higher level.
6. Pay the price to *evaluate*—it will return to you far more than you spent!

4

The Greatest Mover—
The "Mission"!

Preview...

Begin your mission by selling yourself lock, stock, and barrel on the results. That insight will build great momentum along the way. The goal will always be seen as greater than the obstacles that are certain to come.

Understand at the beginning that strength comes from the goal. For the businessperson the mission launches us with enthusiasm, but the problems deflate the balloon that launched us.

The housewife fails to see the great mission of raising the children because of the endless homebound details it brings. The husband also loses the greater mission as fishing, golf, and TV ballgames accumulate. She sees what his problems are while he fails to recognize hers.

The _mission_ of family must be seen as greater than the individual preferences. Sell yourself on the greater mission!

$\mathcal{T}$he _mission_ is the special task for which a person is destined in life. It transcends one's own personal agenda. Thus, as the Bible puts it: "For what should it profit a man, if he shall gain the whole world, and lose his own soul?" (Mark 8:36).

The mission can be very personal, designed for yourself or your whole family. The mission can be a corporate venture for your own company or your employer. Whether one or both, when the mission has been stated and you have agreed to commit time, effort, and perhaps your lifetime toward it, the mission will move you. You will find yourself *pushing_yourself!*

The mission for a housewife, during the child-bearing years, may be summed up simply as "my husband and my kids." And almost every day is a day full of mission; she is dedicated to raising the children and loving her husband. The husband's mission may center on supplying the funds needed for their joint mission for several years to come. But, that's all right, for what could you name as a greater mission?

It may be careers for both, with children coming later, but whatever it is the mission will be the item that dominates the couple's time and effort. So, if you are in the family mission now, what is the definition of your family goals and dreams? That is the mission. As in the life of Jesus, the Bible tells us, "And Jesus increased in wisdom and stature, and in favour with God and man." Luke 2:52. That is what we call balance, and it is part of a man and wife's goal or mission in raising their young family. It's a major mission in life! When the wife also has to work outside the home, there will be adjustments to the mission, even if it does become harder to balance.

When the mission is not certain, it becomes hard to commit to it. When there is no real passion behind the effort, it becomes only a job for a paycheck. If I become satisfied that my work for a living is not going to be my passionate mission, then what else will become my great mission in life?

Even though my day job may take a high percentage of my time, there can still be a higher purpose in life (the mission)! For example, I believe some have been gifted by their Creator with skills for the marketplace. They have developed and honed those skills to a high-paying level. The end purpose of providing excessive incomes (not the mission) will in turn provide for the mission they are so passionate about.

We see this in some of the millionaires of today. In his excellent book *Goals!*, Brain Tracy states these facts:

"In the year 1900, there were five thousand millionaires in America. By the year 2000, the number of millionaires had increased to more than five million, most of them self-made, in one generation. Experts predict that another ten to twenty million millionaires will be created in the next two decades."

Professional athletes are known for their millionaire salaries. In their short careers of ten to fourteen years, they have accumulated millions of dollars more than they will ever spend in a lifetime. That's not a negative. The positive comes when some use their "extras" for a worthwhile project for humanity (the mission). The mission now exceeds the honors and fame of the game or even the wealth accumulated to care for his family and their families to come. There is something greater than self; it's that mission that is now in sight because of the funds available.

Our world is full of those who excel in riches only to squander it all away on themselves and their short-lived friends. There seems to be no mission greater than themselves.

In some sports, we are now approaching a level where some players are close to earning one million dollars per game. A football quarterback will soon be able to throw four interceptions in a game, fumble twice, make no touchdowns, get "booed" off the field, and still receive a million dollars for playing half a game.

Every time I drive past the St. Jude's Hospital in Memphis, my heart aches from knowing that it's full of precious little children who are, at that moment, fighting for their very lives. Parents are there and will not leave until every possibility is exhausted (the mission).

There are hundreds of dedicated staff, nurses, technicians, researchers, and doctors who have given themselves to the mission. We all know of Danny Thomas, who has given and influenced far more funds for this great work than could otherwise be raised. They are *pushing themselves*!

I can remember as a boy in the hills of Tennessee watching the Danny Thomas show. He kept us watching and laughing with his family humor. I'm sure it must have been exciting to be a television star as well as having the income it provided. In some way, he was exposed to a greater purpose in life than a larger house than the last one. The financial ability given to him led to a much greater mission, that of St. Jude's! A great part of his life made him *push himself* to this goal!

Making millions in order to reach worthy goals is not the problem; that is good. Doing so for the destruction of good is a problem. Running drug cartels, the sweatshops of the world, and child pornography rings and the killing of unborn babies for the sake of convenience and many others for the sake of the dollar are the opposite of decent and moral missions. They are not missions but destruction.

So, what would be your greatest mission?

To conclude, what is so significant that it becomes our mission in life? What are we concluding is worth *pushing ourselves* for?

To us, the mission must be accompanied by our goals to accomplish the mission. One step toward the multiple other steps it takes becomes our driving force for a lifetime. Steps become our plan, our strategy, and our daily and weekly actions that move us consistently to the mission. The fulfillment of the next step reloads the gun that shoots us toward the next.

As each step draws us closer to the mission, our energy level increases, and that pushes us to finish another item on the to-do list. Within that list lies another step toward the mission. It's working! I'm actually *pushing myself!* Intentional self-motivation becomes a lifestyle. As we *push ourselves* to achieve the mission, our influence will gain momentum and followers.

Rejoice when the mission for your life is in view. You are far above the norm. Life takes on a greater urgency. Fulfillment fills your life and family.

So, if that mission is there, I can get up every day and say to myself, "Abb, push yourself!"

"But, my arthritis is acting up today."

"Yes, I know, but it's always acting up. So, grin and bear what you must bear and move on!"

Finish your to-do list today. *Push yourself!* Decide early this morning what goes off your to-do list and onto your not-to-do list. *Push yourself!* What needs to be finished today? *Push yourself!* What needs to be delegated to another? Do it! *Push yourself!* Read a chapter of that new book! *Push yourself!* Get up an hour earlier this week to spend five extra hours writing that new lesson or book! *Push yourself!* Read over again your purpose for the mission. *Push yourself!*

You have one life to live, and today is it. You'll never relive today again. The goal in every great day of life is to *push yourself* toward the mission!

I recall a notable athlete who when interviewed and asked about his millions said, "I already have more money than my family, my kids' families, and their kids' families could possibly spend in a lifetime." Now, fifteen years later, the millions are still pouring in. For this athlete I have yet to hear of the mission greater than the accumulation of wealth.

The key thought here is, whether we have the millions or far, far less, what is that main mission in life? Money lasts for a time, but the mission, if big enough, will continue to move your family and others long after you are gone. Making the millions is not the problem, as it can become the necessity needed to inspire and equip a greater mission than ever dreamed before! The lifetime given, the effort extended, and the sacrifices made for that greater than self mission will forever be worth it all! It will always make you *push yourself!*

There is something that moves us, impassions us, energizes us, fulfills us, and sustains us for the lifetime we are given. We call that the mission!

For me and my wife, the mission has been to turn the hearts of children toward their wonderful Creator. For forty-two years and counting, my thoughts, dreams, plans, and innovative drive has been children and teens. My mission now includes teaching the adults who teach all ages.

For a Christian, the surrender of one's life to Christ brings the surrender to His mission, known in scripture as the Great Commission, or simply as we're referring to it here as the mission, in the Bible (Matthew 28:19–20; Acts 16:15). To that mission I give my life, my abilities, my energy, my all. You can see some of the results on masterclubs.org and now trainingteachers.org.

But what is your mission in life? Take time to evaluate your past, your present, and your dreams for the future. Perhaps you have already achieved several dreams or high goals you set at an earlier age. Perhaps all is still well with you and yours, but that driving passion is not there like it used to be. We may need to redefine our mission, which will renew the passion! I need that greater goal in life that causes me to be willing to *push myself!*

I just took a break and took our granddaughter, age five, to the park for swings and slides and more. This beautiful young girl has now created another *mission* for us that involves her alone.

Politicians, which are a scary subject, have a variety of passions that push them every day. Interviews, committees, proposals, receptions, parties, and news conferences all make up their day, with most minutes each day tied into their *mission*. And don't forget, they have a brand new day to spend America's money - yours and mine.

I need not remind you of the corruptions that come with money, power and position. However, we also hear of great gain from the arena of politics. The mission, for good or for self-gain, is what drives this group of national servants. They have attained a level of influence that few have, which can push them and others to a larger mission than most. We listen and watch each night as their mission is paraded before the world.

In the Christian arena, we are seeing more people set their mission for the mission fields of the world at a much older age than ever before. Even some at the ages of fifty, fifty-five, sixty, and sixty-five are heading to the field. Why? Because a greater mission than just retirement burns within them.

These mature men and women have already had their careers and finished that time of their lives. They have made their money, raised their families, started their retirement, and now are beginning to think about their "senior" years. Those years may be short or long, but inside their hearts yearn for doing something greater. Thus, for many, their mission is set to do something great for their God before they go to meet Him! They are willing to *push themselves!*

The ideal is to start early in our career so that a lifetime of commitment will pay the greatest of dividends when the years of toil are over. The mission, throughout my lifetime, would generate all of this:

The mission generates enthusiasm.

The mission generates a commitment to the long haul, if need be.

The mission generates desire to excel in each successive step.

The mission generates your greatest innovative thoughts.

The mission generates the energy you will need to take you there.

It seems as though the routine affairs of life, although necessary and our duty, fall somewhat short of being that greater mission in life. Why am I here? Where am I going? What is my daily purpose? Where is my ultimate end? What could be my chief mission in life?

Understanding some of those questions is what sets the goal and what will push us to that mission! Why would we seek less?

Key Thoughts to Remember/Action Tips

1. How long has it been since reviewing or redefining your major mission for life?
2. Schedule time at least once a week to read your mission statement. One sentence statements are often the best. They are easy to understand and remember.
3. What can I do this week to *push myself* toward the mission's next step? What and to whom can I delegate a part?
4. Look for momentum and use it to celebrate your progress!
5. Is everyone totally clear on their part in the mission?

5

Influence Pushes Others Longer Than You Can Live!

Preview...

A hundred years from now, the accumulation of things that I possessed before I died will not matter. But the world and the eternal world may be different because I went after a child that no one else would go after, and it made the greatest difference in his life!

Influence! You've come this far with someone else's influence. Now it's your turn to influence the next generation!

The influence you have in raising the next generation, for good or for bad, will be your greatest remembered legacy. Your influence can change other people's lives for the rest of their lives. It can be for good or for bad. Influence can build or destroy. Influence can make you well remembered or hated.

Being a role model has been called the greatest unconscious form of learning. I have seen it over and over in the lives of young people. Bullies influence others to become bullies. Peer pressure influences large age groups. Boring teachers influence kids to despise the classroom. Cliques influence small groups for good or bad. Influence exists in the toddler's classroom where follow the leader is so common—"Do what I do."

Webster's New World Dictionary defines influence in this way: "The power of persons or things to affect others. The effect of such power. The power of a person or group to produce effects without the use of force or authority."

So, was it a parent, grandparent, older sibling, teacher, coach, close friend, pastor, or someone else whose influence you most remember? I can immediately pick out a negative and two positive influences from my life. In all probability, you could name scores of people who have been used to "produce effects without the use of force or authority."

My three examples go back to my high school days, and yet I still remember both the negative and the positive influences—and that was fifty-five years ago. I can remember it all in great detail.

The first was my English teacher. Raised in the southern "hills," English wasn't a high priority. When you know kids with names like Elrod, Burford, Bubba, Dudd, Othar, Mutt, Snake, and Essie Bell, you are already being raised with your own "mountain mama's" definitions of words.

But back to my "American English" teacher. This dear lady initiated it all. She asked me to arrive thirty minutes before school to meet with her to allow for extra tutoring in my least favorite subject. I can still remember the serious and sincere expressions on her face as she tried to prepare me to pass the course.

Without her effort, time, and influence, I would not have played football or basketball for academic reasons. I saw early in the morning little tears in her eyes as she tried to *push me!* And she did! I will never forget Mrs. Goldston.

My football coach missed the influence factor. No, we were not a powerhouse team, coming from a town of about three hundred that included the country folks. But none of us wanted to lose, and all of us were willing to improve. Yet, we practiced barely two hours a day.

After coach went home, some of us (teenagers) would stay another two hours running wind sprints and pass plays. The coach literally took my playbook for ideas each year for our plays. I made up football plays with blocking assignments and such during study hall. I don't know what other students did, but I made up my own little world of football. Each year he would ask me for my playbook (a teenager's playbook). He then selected ten to fifteen plays, and those were the plays that we used most of that year. I definitely was not a young Vince Lombardi in the making. His influence wasn't much. Needless to say, we struggled.

My basketball coach was the exact opposite. We practiced four hours a day and ran a hundred laps up and down both sides of the bleachers before each practice. If you missed a day of practice for any reason, you ran an extra one hundred laps after practice or you didn't come back. Tough? Yeah, but winning toughness!

Techniques, skills, dribbling, shooting, passing, team play—it was all there. He gave us books to read, plays to study, mind drills, and we had great discussions about basketball. The fundamentals are what he wanted. We won most of our games! Influence turned us into winners. The value of hard practices, disciplined bodies, and a winning attitude influenced us to play above our natural ability.

Oddly, my two coaches were brothers.

If the one or the several who influenced you did so for the good, then take it now to a higher level and make it count in your life and in the lives of others. Life is not just about you but also about how many others you can influence for good. When I die, my influence for good or bad hangs around for many years. Who will follow you now, and who will feel your influence for years to come? Those are big questions.

The Negative Results of Negative Influence

Gangs influence young kids to go astray. One ringleader in an elementary school can lead many younger children to cheat (as he does), to lie, to steal, and to curse. Ballplayers influence those who love sports. Add up the TV commercials of beer, casinos, poker, and the egos of the so-called stars. Add in the talk shows, R-rated movies, and the sitcoms where many are designed around one-liners where "you put me down, and I'll return the favor." Add in the devastating influence of MTV on very young lives, our humanistic society, the anti-God comedy shows, and don't forget the filthy adult cartoon shows that are watched by more children than adults.

Should we not have a bleak future for our children because of these influences every day of their lives?

A flyer from our son's public school announced that their program for prom night featured a "casino room." They brought in the roulette wheel, black jack tables, and poker for this fun night. It's just for fun and just for fun prizes. Where's the influence? Everyone wins at the casino games! Casino games are fun! Think how great it will be when you can go, and it won't be long!

Influence seeks to begin a lifestyle. Influence is eating the hearts out of our children. Yet, good influence will always triumph when it finds the heart of a child, a teenager, or even an adult. Make a difference in this world with your influence. It's much more fulfilling to build up than to tear down! There's enough to *push yourself!*

I can think back in my ministry to when we would often take teens to downtown Chattanooga to our mission. This was where our church tried to make a difference for the street people, the alcoholics, and the homeless. Hundreds of thousands of dollars were put into that effort over the years. We gave them a nice bath place, a bed, full meals, clean clothes and shoes, encouragement, and, of course, the message that Christ can change lives.

Why take teens to a place where alcohol is heavy on the breath, the smell is awful, and men and women in their thirties look as though they're in their late fifties? Their hands shake, their families have suffered from neglect, and most had already lost their families. We took our teens there for show and smell, hoping to show them where this trail ends for many. Every one of the adults there would tell you it began with that first drink.

Why show teens this end-of-the-line lifestyle? For influence. Negative influence can also teach a powerful lesson. Hopefully, that picture of real life bad lives will be a long-remembered picture that will influence those young lives just heading down the trail.

The Influence of Your Encouragement!

From early childhood, thousands of children are raised to expect defeat. How many of our educators experience kids with all the symptoms of failure? Encouragement has obviously been neglected. Dreams, which are often the greatest in childhood, have all been squelched in their own homes. I wonder how many students teachers see each year who are dreamless because of someone else's influence for the worse? Without encouragement, it will be a delayed achievement for most of them. However, with an intercessor, like you, the sky is still the limit. There is hope for many to come out of their shells. There is hope, but someone needs to intercede as soon as possible.

True encouragement is what everyone deserves. Perhaps, rather than stopping to smell the roses, we could stop long enough to look and listen to the people around us. Our influence must be put into action. Good attitude without action still equals no progress.

Expressions from faces can often wave a red flag in our direction. "Help me," the cry comes. Not from spoken words, but through facial expressions.

We all immediately recognize names like Abraham Lincoln, Woodrow Wilson, Benjamin Franklin, Thomas Jefferson, Helen Keller, John F. Kennedy, Albert Einstein, and Walt Disney. The influence list is inexhaustible.

The average person will not have his or her name remembered around the world, but each person's influence will be remembered through family, grandkids, business, church, and civic groups. Influence counts, for good or bad, and always for a long time. If you spoke at your own funeral, what would you say? What would you say without exaggerating or even lying? Influence is made during that little dash between the years of birth and death on your tombstone. What happened during that time that will still influence those who hear your name?

Influence will apply to others positively, negatively, or perhaps, worst of all, there will be no good influence at all. Influence stirs others into following your lead.

Influence makes you a hero to young learners. Influence draws customers. Influence puts your name at the head of their lists. All of life is affected by influence!

When considering our influence, there is *now* and there is *later*. I must *push myself* in order to increase my influence both now and later. With a greater influence now than in my younger years, influence is kept alive today and will build a greater case for tomorrow.

At the age of seventy-two, my long-range major goals have shortened from the fifteen- to twenty-year spans to more like five-year goals. Shooting for five more years of life, if God allows, brings a greater urgency for achievement. As a younger man, I couldn't picture myself dying, other than by some accident. My goals were long-term, but that long-term is now here.

Looking at the possibility of life for five more years creates an urgency to *push myself!* I can get pumped up thinking how realistic my productive life just may be. Oh, it's not a morbid outlook on life, but an optimistic and realistic understanding that every day carries more importance than ever before!

I must increase my performance and my output to increase my influence. What my influence is accomplishing now should be greater because of the years of experience. The years of experience in honing my skills should have some good value to those who follow. That is influence, always striving, always increasing in knowledge and wisdom and understanding. I trust that's your goal. Your influence may be one hundred times greater than mine. I hope so. That will also become your level of responsibility, to keep it untarnished!

A beautiful Bible verse reminds us what is available for those who put their trust in the Lord: "For the Lord giveth wisdom: out of his mouth cometh knowledge and understanding" (Proverbs 2:6).

Yesterday, in one of my teacher training sessions, there was an eighty-two-year-old lady in attendance. Sitting in the front row, she repeatedly said, "Amen," when I made a strong point about a principle of teaching. No one else did, but she did. You could see it in her eyes: the passion, the enthusiasm, and the anticipation of learning something new. Why is it always those in their late seventies or early eighties, having taught already for sixty years, who have the greatest zeal? I think she too may be living on the short-term goals of three to five years. She still burns within to achieve more. By the talk of those who know her best, her influence is already strong today. She has learned to *push herself!*

Our influence will be seen through our performance. If our performance improves, so will our influence now and later. If our striving begins the downward slide, so does our influence. Our disinterest in our performance has only one direction to go, and it's not up. That's why learning early on to *push yourself* is what keeps your mind active and your willpower alive. Someone said, "When you're through improving, you're through." There's a way to avoid this tragedy, by learning to *push yourself!*

In *The Laws of Lifetime Growth*, Sullivan and Nomura state:

> "Continually work to surpass everything you've done so far, and your performance will always be greater than your applause. . . . The goal here is always to be getting better; to appreciate how far you've come, but also to keep striving to go further, always making your future bigger than your past".

What great advice! This powerful book should be in your library to read and reread.

The only interest I have with the past is the part that might make me better than today. When I fail to evaluate the past, I lose all that experience that could add wisdom for the future. If I live only from my past achievements, then the only influence I'm spreading is from years past. The problem is, I'm not dead yet. What about the future? Where is the wisdom, knowledge, and understanding that makes me so valuable for today? Age should not begin a slide in my influence, but should enhance my influence for today! I should be of greater worth now than in my younger years. Whether or not you are a technical genius with today's "tools"; wisdom, knowledge, and understanding supersede most accessories. Add the technical skills, and it will add much gain for you. In businesses they often "hire their weaknesses".

Your greater influence is tied best to that purpose you have. Your gifts and skills developed toward your ultimate purpose in life is your top shelf. When the rabbit trails of life have been kept to a minimum, with time and effort spent on your main purpose (your dream, goal, objective), then you still have much to offer, and your influence is still on the rise. That's what I want, and that's what I can have if I will keep on *pushing myself!*

Think of the future and your influence will continue to expand! Spend most of your time continuing to enhance your gifts, your talents, and your abilities. These areas represents the best you have to offer. Others are more gifted in different areas. We too often want to become what we are not gifted to become. Oh, we could do it, but with less interest, less intensity, and less skill than someone who is gifted in that area. Because of your giftedness, you will always excel in one area more than others. It comes more natural. Your excitement and energy peaks faster. The results are always a notch above average. That's where you shine. And that's where your influence will be greater. When you exceed expectations, others are influenced by you. That's a great feeling, and there's *your push!*

The Influence of the Word of God!

Nothing compares with the truth you have learned when it is applied to the lives of students whom you will seek to influence. Your passion must be catching!

Your role is to so clarify what God has to say so that the student cannot possibly miss what God has to say. That's who a teacher is and what a teacher does. Your influence, using what you've been trained to use, is far above your own personal influence. Continue your study. Continue your knowledge of methods and techniques in order to apply the truth you now know. The Word changes lives now and forever. That's the ultimate influence, and God can use someone like you to be a teacher worth listening to. May God be glorified through you!

Passion Can Become Great Encouragement!

Teachers should be a constant source of encouragement. So should we all. Everyone needs encouragement. The confident person increases his chances to succeed. Encouragement lifts up, builds up, and fires up all ages!

Passion Is Seen by Great Faith!

The gifts and calling of God are permanent and enduring. Romans 11:29 tells us, "For the gifts and calling of God are without repentance." In this verse "repentance" means irrevocable. Even if we have never done anything with the gifts and abilities given to us, even if we have failed over and over, God's gifts and calling are still resident within us.

Yes, even senior saints still have much potential left. Your skills are now perfected skills with much more good potential than when you first started!

In scripture, a lack of faith always bothered Jesus. Jesus never reproved his disciples for a lack of wealth or intelligence or talents, but He did for a lack of faith. Our faith needs to be big enough for our children and grandchildren to see. Great faith influences everyone around you!

Here's a thought: are my many years of experience and talents that have been perfected *still* available to God? The center of God's will doesn't conclude when retirement begins! Influence, even yours, is what the whole world needs, so give it at every opportunity and with a greater passion than in the past. *There's your push!*

Key Thoughts to Remember/Action Tips

1. List three high goals for your life that would leave an influence for others who follow:

   a. _____

   _____

   b. _____

   _____

   c. _____

   _____

2. Start with your own family. What is it they are picking up from your life? Brainstorm to refresh the good and the bad of your habits that others see as a way to live.
3. From the spiritual side, what do your children see in you that is attractive to them?
4. Do your children see effort, initiative, and hard work or gentleness, kindness, goodness, and love for God or none of the above? Influence—it's the you that really is seen by others.

6
Developing Strategy Gives Me The Green Light!

Preview...

Growing up in the hills of Tennessee, our family planned to go to Florida for many years, yet rarely traveled beyond the county line. We actually thought that was special. The dream was there, but the plans never made the calendar. It was a dream without a deadline. Strategy, in its simplest form, becomes my steps to the goal. One giant step is too big for most. Too many steps dim the vision too. Goals need the intermediate steps, but goals also need a deadline. Strategy is general planning for how to proceed. Tactics become your en route maneuvers that keep the course straight!

Strategy pushes me because strategy brings *clarity* to the project ahead. It proves to me, on paper, that my project or goal is well within reach. That alone turns the red light to green!

It begins, of course, with my purpose or objective. Once I have the ideal outcome clearly in mind, it's time to strategize *how* I'm going to pull it off. Strategy becomes the way I will deliver the goods. It's not the vision or purpose or goal itself, but strategy becomes the methods, the techniques, the steps en route to the mission, the goal, or the ultimate destination.

Immediately, I can see how valuable such planning is. So, whatever time it takes to think it through, run it by my fellow workers, critique it, ask enough "What if . . ." questions, and exhaust all scenarios possible, be assured that time is worth it all. Always *push yourself* to plan well.

For a teacher, strategy is your content and how you place it in a step-by-step logical sequence. It's planning the step of classroom involvement, the step to illustrate in real life, or the step of defining words. The Bible story step will picture the truth in a real-life scenario that my age group can identify with. So, in the ideas I give here, listen for a thought here and there, write it down, and add a step to help you in your lesson preparation.

Strategy is not a technical word above your reach to understand or to apply. It is the way you get to where you want to go. You are simply writing down the steps to your goal or your dream. Strategy is your preplanning in order to make your mistakes on paper, not through the school of hard knocks.

You have often heard the saying "Failing to plan is planning to fail." It's a simple thought, but close to absolutely right. Strategy helps you to cross bridges before you get there and well worth the time spent.

Tactics, on the other hand, become your in-battle maneuvers once you are in route to the goal. For a teacher, the tactics may need to change as you watch the mannerisms of your students and see a distinct noninterest or an obvious restlessness. Change something before it gets worse!

Military strategists often mention that the best of strategies only gets everyone on the same page and all moving toward the same objective. Strategy generates the energy and enthusiasm but is always open to changes along the way (the maneuvers to the left or right.) It's the tweaks that keep us on course. However, without that initial strategy, we tend to all go off in our own directions.

For example, our ministry to children is called Master Clubs. Hundreds of churches use this ministry as a major part of the curriculum for children from ages three through sixth grade.

This is our purpose statement:

> To evangelize children, discipling them for spiritual growth, teaching them God's truth, training them to serve Jesus

Christ, and to provide multiple opportunities to do so in and through our church.

Evangelize—Disciple—Teach—Train—Provide Opportunities

Well, that all sounds good, but exactly what do we do?

For our home-base ministry to their church ministry, it should certainly tie together. So, for Master Ministries, the umbrella name for all we do, with Master Clubs as the biggest part, our role is to supply other churches with the training and all the curriculum. Therefore, the purpose statement could be fulfilled in their own church. In other words, if you use our program, we will help you in multiple ways to evangelize, disciple, teach, train, and provide opportunities.

For Master Ministries, our job is just that. The strategy for the most part was done in the past as this entire ministry grew up over the past thirty-five years. Our strategy today continues but is centered on helping hundreds of churches who work under different leadership, finances, worker experience, facilities, and other unique circumstances.

A large goal then for Master Ministries is in training these churches to adjust, to modify if needed, but to still keep the basic objectives as their goal. If the statement of purpose cannot be implemented in your church, then you don't need Master Clubs. We can help you to adapt, but what we have to offer is all consumed in the words "evangelize, disciple, teach, train, and provide opportunities."

In future years, whatever we may add to our warehouse of materials will still tie into the original purpose statement to be true to our mission.

Strategy for us is to keep enhancing materials and training. If another step or another product will do that, then we produce it. So, the same strategy put into place thirty-five years ago still pushes us to get better at what we do today. Our goal is to specialize in children's ministry. We desire to be a brand name in children's ministry!

All the above is what *pushes us*! There's a reason now to stay up later or get up earlier in order to someday supply thousands of churches with exactly what they need! Great purpose leads to great energy and enthusiasm to reach the goal.

So, what is it that *pushes me* to get up an hour earlier in the morning in order to get another hour out of my day? What is it that demands hours of strategy as I try to get it right the first time?

Strategy *pushes me!* Because from those hours spent will come my best answer, my best solution, and my best workable plan! Once that initial thinking it through phase is complete, I can then spend my time working my plan and allowing for some in-battle maneuvering. Full speed ahead! That *pushes me!* When the green light flashes, it's time to put the pedal to the metal!

Strategy pushes you to be both realistic and futuristic. Strategy will bring vision into focus. Often the details seem so minute for some leaders. Yet the details are often the only difference between an excellent and a mediocre project.

Strategizing is the *preplanning* for those details to take shape. Adjustments (tactical maneuvers) will always be needed, but your preplanning (strategy) will get the action going. That *pushes me* to set it all in motion!

Strategy will move you in the right direction. Strategy takes a big issue and breaks it into manageable sizes to farm out to fellow workers. Strategy is my steps to the goal. When I plan on paper, I can see my goal well in sight. That *pushes me! Push yourself!*

Written strategy helps me see possible pitfalls, blockades, or detours ahead. Laying out additional options helps me to choose another road before I get there. That *pushes me* to keep on thinking for that better route!

Strategy helps you to *visualize* taking on a project that is probably above your comfort zone. Because you can see it on paper, it brings the confidence you need to move ahead. It will reduce error and solve many problems before they arrive. That gives me confidence, assurance, and *pushes me! "Now unto him that is able to do exceeding abundantly above all that we ask or think, according to the power that worketh in us".*
—Ephesians 3:20

Strategizing *makes you think.* It makes you focus your thinking on the target. It makes you ask yourself the right questions. *Push yourself!*

Strategy gets me on the right path. Whether I lead the group or the project or teach a class of junior boys, strategy solves lots of problems ahead of time! The architect solves problems before they arrive. The business consultant reminds you to see what you overlooked before you get there. The doctor can save your life before you forfeit it.

Strategy is simply your plan, system, structure, or program that gives specific planned direction toward the goal in mind. If every worker does his own thing, who knows what has actually been accomplished or what has been overlooked or ignored? Strategy gets you *organized*! Realizing that you could be the person to point everyone else toward the goal should *push you!*

Start simple by listing your objectives. Add to the list as time goes by. If your strategy sessions brought up twenty good objectives to accomplish, then what are the ten best? Now, narrow that to the best five of the ten. Now, go a step further by choosing the best two of the final five. Now, choose one and go with it. If it falters, I still have four more from the best five of the twenty. Can you feel the excitement that gives to a leader? That *pushes me* to launch out and set the sails high to the wind!

When purpose (what we do) is clear, how to accomplish that purpose is clear and every decision moves in that direction. That's what strategy is. It is defining *what* we plan to do (the ultimate goal), then strategizing *how* we plan to do *what* we plan to do. What will it take? What tools do I need? Do I need to purchase some items or make some myself? Do I have enough leaders to make it happen? The *where* we do it, or the time slot, comes next. In most cases, it doesn't matter where or when it is accomplished, as long as it will happen somewhere at some time!

When your period of strategizing is complete, you will feel a rush of energy and enthusiasm kick in. *There's your push!*

7

Decisiveness Gets Me Off The Dime!

Preview...

(Indecisive) It's the honey-do list that is three months old.

(Indecisive) It's the golfer that cringes on every tee shot.

(Indecisive) It's the family argument where neither side will bend.

(Indecisive) It's the classroom problem that seems to last forever.

All would go away if someone would get off the dime.

The dime makes for a very small spot. I need the space to roam if I intend to go further than I have thus far. Decisiveness brings me to a decision.

A dime makes for a very small spot and doesn't cover much ground. I need to move off the "dime" to finish my course!

*T*he inability to make decisions can close down your operation. It can stop all progress. It can drain the interest in those ready to help. It can greatly limit your accomplishments.

Now, turn it around. The ability to make decisions in a timely manner can eliminate all the above. It can prosper all your undertakings! So, *push yourself* to be a decisive person.

Instead of waiting for other people or circumstances to decide for me, I can make things happen by being decisive. We can keep our goals in sight and reach for them through decision making. If you are a teacher, then most decisions are up to you because no one teaches your particular students but you. Decisiveness will put your lesson together in plenty of time to master your notes!

Some Observations

Years ago I read that we should not stop thinking when the first good answer emerges because usually a better idea comes soon. It's happened for me over and over. That must mean you should seek all the knowledge you can before closing down your options. You must have options because there is usually a better one that comes when you keep thinking. However, there does come the time to stop the option hunting and to decide on your best two. Now, choose one (decisiveness) and go with it.

Most decisions require follow-up, usually as soon as possible. It's easy to say "that's my decision," but that is really only the starting place for action. So, it's not the option I choose but the follow-up that brings the value to that choice.

When a decision is made, it lifts your spirit. It energizes you. It makes you feel like a new person. It makes you want to tackle whatever comes next.

Brainstorming by yourself or, even better, with others may bring ten to fifteen or more options to consider. Bring those down to the best five and then to one or two. Choose one and go with it. It's good to have others in on your option hunt. Often, someone else will take your idea and raise it to a higher level. Welcome all the ideas you can think of.

> *"A decision is a judgment. It is a choice between*
> *alternatives. It is rarely a choice between right or wrong.*
> *It is often a choice between two courses of action, neither . . .*
> *more nearly right than the other."*
> — Peter Drucker

When indecisiveness rears its head, go to your think time! That is where you are able to get back to reality and the starting place for improvement. Use the age-old technique of asking yourself some key and sometimes difficult questions and then making yourself come up with an answer. After all, if you don't know the answer, who does? Practice thinking. *Push yourself!*

Ask questions like these: Does this need a decision right now? Do I have all the facts in hand? Who can help me with a clear picture? Does someone else have the authority to handle this? Is what's needed a one-time clear answer from the boss? Will one step clear this problem or will it take steps? Who will do the steps? Who will do the follow-up and determine whether the problem is resolved or not? What if we just let it ride until it clears itself? List your consequences to the options stated.

> *"Every decision is like surgery. It is an intervention into a system and therefore carries with it the risk of shock. One does not make unnecessary decisions any more than a good surgeon does unnecessary surgery".*
> —Peter Drucker

Force yourself to take a good hard look at the *risks* and the *consequences*. These are two big words that those who manage must have a good working understanding of before getting too far off base. To get caught off the safety of the base becomes an out. If you want to risk it, then risk it. Sometimes the consequences of the risk either win the game for you or lose it. But someone has to take risks occasionally. If your gut feeling gives you that uneasy feeling inside, your intuition is probably signaling that the risk is too great this time. Next time the same risk could feel good, so you go for it. Leaders can never live out their lives on easy street. If decisiveness is called for, then that is who you are and what you do!

Write Down Your Plan to Get Moving

With little experience working with teenagers, having come from a much smaller church to a church of over five thousand, I suddenly found myself as the youth director of that very large church and all those teens after only one year. The only thing I knew how to do was to think it through. So, out came one piece of blank paper. I put about seven or eight squares on it and sat there thinking and staring at the blank page. Little by little, I tried picking an area for teens (curriculum, memory, service, evangelism, etc.) and began to lay out some options. Don't ask me how many wadded-up pieces of paper flew toward the trash can.

Over and over again, this process has been my way. Thoughts on paper, over and over. Finally, there's my plan! There's *my push!*

Come Out of Planning with Steps Laid Out!

Steps will keep you on track. Steps will give you assurance. Steps will put your workload in manageable sizes to farm out to your workforce. Workers can handle small steps, though those same workers often have problems with giant steps. They can't see as far as you can see into the future. They don't need to.

Find a time slot for each step. Go to your calendar. As each day rolls around, it must appear somewhere on your daily agenda. Sometimes a one-hour time slot will *push you* more than a three-hour slot. Schedule three one-hour slots, giving breathers in between for duties with less pressure lower on your list. You probably already know what would work best for you.

Personally, I like to award myself for accomplishing tasks (because no one else will). For example, if I have a great hour of getting off the dime and seeing progress made, my reward is a thirty-minute slot to work on a book—like this one. That's what drives me! There's *my push!*

However, you may be different. I've known some who will honor themselves with a chocolate bar for reaching a goal. Others have used milkshakes, a new tie, or a trip to the Bass Pro Shop. One of the ultimate awards is to give yourself thirty minutes to watch another Barney Fife rerun!

Stand Tall and Tackle the Difficult!

We probably all have some part of a project that just keeps getting pushed to the back burner. We procrastinate.

In his book, *Time Power*, Brian Tracy records sixteen ways to move yourself to avoid procrastination. He shows us how to get off the dime. One of his sixteen ideas says this: "Resist the tendency toward perfectionism. Since perfectionism is a major reason for procrastination, decide not to worry about doing the job perfectly. Just get started and work steadily."

Wonderful advice! Your aggressiveness toward the next step of the project will influence others who are watching you lead. You are teaching, you are training, and you are inspiring all those who follow you on the steps to achievement!

Little Victories (the Everyday Kind) Build Momentum!

Build momentum for winning! Little steps come much more often than the long-range bigger achievements. You need something to celebrate often! Little steps toward the overall project can become as significant for your workforce as waiting for weeks or months to announce a bigger win. Everyone needs encouragement almost every day. It doesn't have to be a gigantic or stupendous step that we finished. Obviously that's a big win, but that kind of progress may be six months away. I need that everyday or once-a-week momentum-builder win that our team can share. That's what moves people today toward the greater goal down the road.

Did we have a good week? Then, please tell me. I will come back on Monday anticipating another good week! That's momentum, and momentum *pushes us all!*

Is There a Sense of Urgency?

If there is no sense of urgency, you may just find yourself only slightly motivated. But that can't be because you're the leader. Your drive, your determination, your sense of *now* will not only *push yourself* but may be the best push you have for your workforce. If you fall short, they fall short. If you slow the pace, so do they. If you procrastinate, they do too. If the task generates little urgency, then all that motivational momentum is lacking for the whole team, which brings the consequences you do not want.

Go back again and remind yourself of your goal. Look again at what that goal will bring to the project, to your business, and to your ministry. Do some more self-talk. Come back again fired up and let your fellow workers watch you burn with the urgency that demands the whole team strike up their own fires again!

Back in the hills, my dad used a familiar Southern term, "Son, git er' done!" I knew exactly what he meant. After the first time I didn't git er' done, my reward was a hickory switch. The most

59

humiliating part was when Mom made me go out and pick out my own hickory switch that would then be applied to the child in question. Oh, doggies! That got er' done in record time.

In *A Sense of Urgency*, John P. Kotter says this:

> "When people have a true sense of urgency, they think that action on critical issues is needed now, not eventually, not when it fits easily into a schedule. Now means making real progress every single day. Critically important means challenges that are central to success or survival, winning or losing".

That's why your think time will help you to discern your priority list. I'll never get over how hundreds of times my think time brought out the picture so clear that I approached the problem with the anticipation of success. That's a wonderful feeling, and when that feeling is there, it most often proves to be true.

Decisiveness is a mark of leadership. It brings great rewards. Being indecisive will put your goal in slow-motion, and so will be your production. If you see yourself described here as indecisive, *push yourself* to get free. If you are doing pretty well for now, *push yourself* to get even better. Everyone around you will benefit. Intentional self-motivation—we all need it, and we can all have it!

Key Thoughts to Remember/Action Tips

1. What is obsolete or irrelevant that needs to be abandoned? When?
2. Make your list. Your wife may suggest the honey-do list.
3. Pick one or two each week and make your decision.
4. Read a chapter of that new book.
5. What can be delegated to another? Do it!
6. What needs to be finished today? *Push yourself!*
7. Decide the night before what the priority will be for the next day.

8

Evaluation Initiates
Greater Achievement!

Preview...

It works for your career, your dreams, your family, your goals, your ministry, and your personal improvement. It solves lots of problems instantly. It clarifies areas for correction. It crosses bridges before you get there. It improves your position from adequate to excellent. Evaluation checks the scoreboard. Evaluation helps you to face reality. Evaluation is a sign of leadership. Evaluation helps me to check on me!

"Experience doesn't make you better. Only *evaluated* experience makes you better," says Dr. Howard Hendricks.

Evaluation is intentional self-motivation.

*B*ut I don't want to stop and evaluate the project. I don't really want to know if I'm winning or losing. Everything seems to be working. Let's not mess with it. Leave well enough alone. On and on we can go, rationalizing why it's just fine to *assume* we're reaching our goal rather than *facing reality*. That's the negative. Let's get over it and learn to change our thinking.

1. Evaluation Is an Attitude

Evaluation is an attitude of improving my position from adequate to excellent! The better attitude is this: "I can't wait to find a better, more productive way than how we do it now!" That kind of attitude pushes me to schedule evaluation times on my calendar. I really can't wait. What if I could do it better, faster, cheaper, with greater results than ever? Surely I would want to know. That's what awaits at the end of my next evaluation!

We are all one person. We all have our level of incompetence. We are not the Lone Ranger with the capacity to pull off a one-man show.

2. Maintaining Is Not Enough

Maintaining where we are is not the *mission*. There's no push in just maintaining. The drive has settled back into neutral. There's no forward momentum, no greater heights to achieve. I have put myself in a position where I cannot even push myself, much less the others who could help me get there. Evaluation forces me to face reality. I need that to *push me*. I need that to energize me to *push others*.

Salvador Diaz-Verson Jr., quoted in the book *Leadership Secrets of World's Most Successful CEOs* by Eric Yaverbaum, said,

> "If, however a person wishes to become a leader or a better leader, then the process begins by examining one's own skill strengths, moral code, people skills, and big picture abilities. You don't become a better leader by changing other people; you become a better leader by improving yourself. *Evaluation* helps us to take an honest look at our own effectiveness".

3. Evaluation Initiates Greater Achievement

Evaluation initiates greater achievement. You will soon realize that you must let go and allow others to carry the project to the goal. There is great power in letting go. Delegating, but still hanging onto all the details is not enough. The key is in releasing leadership to others.

Jack Welch, former CEO of the GE Corporation, gave these thoughts in his book *Winning*:

> "Rule 1. Leaders relentlessly upgrade their team, using every encounter as an opportunity to evaluate, coach, and build self-confidence. You have to evaluate—making sure the right people are in the right jobs. . . . You have to coach—guiding, critiquing, and helping people to improve their performance in every way. And finally, you have to build self-confidence—pouring out encouragement, caring, and recognition. Self-confidence energizes, and it gives your people the courage to stretch, take risks, and achieve beyond their dreams. It is the fuel of winning teams."

Quoting author Peter Drucker, Marshall Goldsmith, in his book *What Got You Here Won't Get You There,* said of Drucker: "The wisest thing I heard him say, 'We spend a lot of time teaching leaders what to do. We don't spend enough time teaching leaders what to stop. Half the leaders I have met don't need to learn what to do. They need to learn what to stop."

Our ability to delegate often fades over time as we go back again to doing it all ourselves. A not-to-do list is a good practice. Sharing the load is perhaps even better.

4. Evaluation Keeps You From Doing It All

In the Bible, Jesus turned over the responsibility for administering the church to a few former fisherman and tax collectors just three years old in the Lord: "And he ordained twelve, that they should be with him, and that he might send them forth to preach" (Mark 3:14).

Notice the words carefully in verse 14: "with him" and "send them forth." That is still the procedure today. Add to your workforce and send them forth to work. Evaluation reminds you that with more in the workforce the project comes clearer in view. Evaluation often reveals that one person is holding too tightly to many responsibilities. That person may even be you. This possibility pushes me to set up the next evaluation on a regular basis.

Here's a big question: are you willing to give up the credit that used to go to you alone and allow others to be in charge? If not, then you may soon come to your level of incompetence and drift to sleep in a maintenance mode. We all need an *exit plan*. An exit plan is the way you actually reproduce your own leadership as you rearrange your own priorities and duties. Die without a successor to your mission, and it is highly probable the mission dies.

Your leadership is the same as throughout many organizations:

(1) You must be a visionary (dream your dreams)
(2) You must be a fixer (keep plugging your holes)

1. **Evaluation Checks the Scoreboard** We all have the tendency to forge ahead without checking some kind of scoreboard to see if we're actually winning or losing. But, that's evaluation, and you need it. It will push you forward. Satisfaction is the enemy of progress. Satisfaction deadens efforts. Satisfaction seeks no goals. Satisfaction has finished its course. Satisfaction brings no higher goals to achieve.

In the excellent book by John L. Mason, *An Enemy Called Average*, he states: "Dissatisfaction is not the absence of things but the absence of vision." Again, "The quality of your life will be in direct proportion to your commitment to excellence, regardless of what you choose to do."

Certainly we can all find satisfaction in a goal reached, but that satisfaction should push me to a higher more satisfying goal. Allow what could slow you down to actually speed you up. *Push yourself!*

2. Evaluation Needs a Specific Time

Planning to evaluate your work in progress must show up on your calendar. Fear not! Remember, methods or techniques need not be sacred cows. Changing methods is not a sign to everyone you have failed. Your values and your mission should stand the test of time, but methods can change whenever needed. In fact, changing may be the best sign of leadership you can give.

Rethinking your plans is not bad. Things may have changed over time. Assign a think time to design your change for the better.

Think it through again and you'll be glad you did. Years ago, I remember hearing one of the first- or second-year radio broadcasts by Dr. James Dobson as he was beginning his work. He interviewed three CEOs of three of the largest companies in the world. Each talked of the significance of having a think time to solve their problems or cast their visions. Thanks to them, I learned early on to think my way through whatever needed that kind of attention!

3. Evaluation Reveals the Truth

Evaluation helps you to face reality. If you are unable to face the truth, problems seem to last forever. Understanding your bottom line is the difference between where you are and where you could be in two or three years from now!

In his book *Creating Magic*, Lee Cockerell says of his boss,

"Walt Disney didn't wait for employees or customers to complain about hassles before he re-evaluated his processes. As a great leader always should, he looked for ways to improve how things are done because "We've always done it that way" could mean that you've been doing it wrong all along".

The "hassles" referred to *deficient service to guests.*

What are the advantages and disadvantages six months down the road? Evaluation does that! That's what *pushes me* to the next step of my goal!

Sometimes you will need to remove yourself from the middle of the situation, back off, and then take another look from a distance. See the same picture but from a different perspective. Companies often hire consultants for the purpose of a new unbiased set of eyes. Their job is to show us what we can't see!

4. Evaluation Shows the Accumulation Results

Review your objectives and then scan your records to see where reality puts you. Keep good records. Insist on others keeping good records. Records are your lifeline. Records will sit down and have a good talk with you. Records will tell you what's going right or where the problem lies. Maybe it's an employee or staff person who is your weak link. Maybe it's a method that's holding up the production line. Records keep score. Don't you want to look at the scoreboard occasionally? Evaluation does that! The scoreboard pushes me to push on.

Evaluation is a sign of leadership. *It is a leader who anticipates improving.*

Here's a great thought from Dr. Howard Hendricks: "Experience doesn't make you better. Only evaluated experience makes you better." Evaluation means that you have a passion to do a greater work than has been done to date. It's that fire that burns within. It's that drive that will not allow you to slip into a maintenance mind-set.

Evaluation Helps Me to Check on Me.

Am I leading, but no one's following?
Am I teaching, but there's no visible response of learning?
Am I preaching, but nobody sees me doing what I'm preaching?

Evaluation pushes me to take a good long honest look and then change, if need be!

When your expectations run high, the time to evaluate once again is good news. You don't dread it; you look forward to it. "I can't wait till my next think time begins!" Is that your attitude?

5. High Achievers Always Evaluate

Peter Daniels, an internationally acclaimed businessman, when asked what made the difference for him, said: "I schedule time to think. In fact, I reserve one day a week on my calendar just to think. All of my greatest ideas, opportunities and money making ventures started with the days I took off to think!"

If we're not careful, our response might be, "Well, yeah, but I don't have the spare time like a guy who runs eight corporations around the world." Sounds just like one of my own ways of reasoning. Mr. Daniels learned a long time ago to *push himself!*

Dan Cathy, the president of Chick-fil-A, who contributes millions to good causes, lists his thinking schedule (heard on a radio interview):

> 1/2 day every two weeks
> 1 full day each month
> 2–3 full days every year (equals 28 full days a year

He explains, this helps me to keep the main thing the main thing.

6. Evaluation Is Intentional Self-Motivation

Without evaluation, we are destined to repeat our ineffective methods and techniques again and again, even though we know they are not working.

In conclusion, evaluation is *intentional self-motivation*. It is planning spots of time to take stock of what's working and what's not working. If it's not working, then why am I still doing it?

Key Thoughts to Remember/Action Tips

1. You will never appreciate the great value of evaluation until it proves its value to you.
2. Evaluation will reveal what should come off your to-do list and onto a not-to-do list!
3. List a prospect or two who could share the load:

   a. _____

   b. _____

4. Do you have an exit plan for when the project is turned over to another while you advance on to other goals?
5. Get up an hour earlier this week to spend five extra hours on that next step to your goal.

9

Focus Keeps Me On Target!

Preview...

Focus can actually improve our output and our performance. Focus can successfully aid us in being intense in many productive minutes of time. Take a short break with a menial task and then concentrate again.

Focus aims our mind at the core of the project. The strength that focus gives will undoubtedly bring better gain. Focus set on a significant project is the smarter or more productive way!

Focus allows us to avoid making the same mistake multiple times. Focus keeps me from forgetting the details that often make the biggest difference of all.

When leadership is allowed to focus on less, it allows more concentration on that which is critical to the whole. How refreshing to see someone lead an unproductive project back on course!

One of the greatest words you will ever incorporate into your lifestyle is this wonderful word: *focus*. It will change your perspective for good!

We Choose to Narrow Our Focus

Organizations are forever adding to but never subtracting from a multitude of good ideas over the years. One idea is added to another, sucking up more time, resources, energy, finances, and personnel. Our list of good things to do just keeps increasing and never seems to decrease. It's not that new ideas are not in the good category, but as your personnel increases so do the ideas.

A single-minded determination will bring greater focus on your key goal. Now you have more time to adjust and fine-tune your focus. Now, you can *push yourself*, all of yourself, on the target. Wouldn't you enjoy working in one aspect of a company or project or ministry where your role is to become a specialist in that one area? That certainly doesn't mean you are doing less than you are capable of doing, but you are advancing toward being known as an expert in that field.

H. Dale Burke, in his book *Less Is More Leadership*, makes this great statement: "Specialization doesn't mean you are doing less; in fact, you are doing more. But you're doing more of your best stuff instead of just stuff." Then he says, "Many leaders devote most of their energy toward goals that are heavy on maintenance and light on mission."

We Choose to Focus Where We Are Best

Focus keeps you out of those time-robbing projects that come up so quickly and seem so urgent at the moment. I must learn to push them aside in order to *push myself* toward becoming a specialist in the area for which I will be using my best skills continually on the most significant project! Thus, my strengths focused on fewer projects will undoubtedly bring more gain.

Do you have the authority to narrow your focus? Do you have permission to stop doing whatever is not working? It will free you up to focus more on the necessities. Don't be afraid to talk to your superior. He or she does not often walk in your shoes. Share with him or her that you're not looking for less to do but that your goal is to develop your own personal strengths to the point of becoming a specialist. Perhaps they have not looked at you in that light before. Spell it out: the advantages, the time saved, the projects completed with excellence, and how that affects your spirit toward the project.

We must value our time. It's all we have. We'll never live this day again. Today is important, but for exactly what? Whatever is the most significant work to do should be incorporated into my daily agenda. That's your route to becoming a specialist, and as Dale Burke said in his book *Less Is More Leadership*, "now you are not doing less, but actually more, and more of your best stuff!" That's where the focus should remain. Do a few things well to be able to accomplish more things effectively.

Find where people are at their best. Being out of place is like a company putting a $100 an hour worker on a $10 an hour job. It doesn't seem to be getting the best use out of that worker. The more time I spend working on important tasks that bring great dividends in the future, the sooner it will result in more fruit! So, doing fewer projects, with potentially greater results, is doing less in order to do more!

> *Whatsoever thy hand findeth to do, do it with thy might;*
> *for there is no work, nor device, nor knowledge,*
> *nor wisdom, in the grave, whither thou goest.*
> —Ecclesiastes 9:10

We Do Less in Order to Do More

In his book *Less Is More Leadership*, H. Dale Burke states: "Some leaders have 20 years' experience, and others have one year of experience repeated 20 times!" That should never be said of us. We learn to work smarter, not necessarily longer hours. When you focus on those high-dividend projects, greater results will always be forthcoming in the days, weeks, and months ahead! Push yourself to be that committed to focus.

Focus allows us to avoid making the same mistake multiple times. We have probably all done that in some area of life or work.

According to the well-known idea called the Pareto Principle, we see that 20 percent of what we do actually brings 80 percent of the value. By doing less, but the most important less, we actually achieve more in results. This is not a scheme to get out of work, but to work 80 percent smarter. In other words, you can do less, and yet have greater results.

Whatever your major accomplishment is to be, it deserves your greatest effort. Therefore, time and effort on the noncritical areas need to decrease as soon as possible. I believe that the word and meaning of *focus* will be one of the most important words now and thirty years from now.

When we focus, we distinctively define *how* we do *what* we do. Those are the details that must saturate my time, effort, and energy. Your strategy (explained elsewhere) will define *how* you do *what* you do, while the rest makes up the details of your plan.

An example in the area of teaching:

In teaching, the whole idea of teaching *less total content* is that I can then teach the best of it all with better clarity. Now I can focus on words and terms the students might not understand to illustrate or discuss or answer questions to help them to completely grasp what is being said.

I can now personalize the truth through illustrations that strike home. I can now help the learner to see himself in the truth. Now, there's time to emphasize clearly the application into real life and allow time for my students to respond to that truth. Now, it's highly possible that life change and consistent behavior can take place! The more total content you have, the less time you have to focus on anything.

But, if I teach far more content than is even necessary, it becomes all teacher-centered, or another big dose of content with no personal conclusion to the whole matter in the mind of the student. I had nine pages of notes that left me no time to move to student-centered where the only possibility of life change lies. The goal is to teach less for more in order to be grasped more easily by the student. It is to be clear and understandable enough to quickly change the student's life.

Growing up in a very small town in the Tennessee hills, your to-do list wasn't very big to start with. In the summertime, perhaps my job was a list of three items: feed the pig, empty the slop jar, and run the birds out of the garden. Other than that, go play! In other words, go focus on something till supper time.

In talking to others from small towns, one said he was raised in such a small town in Alabama that when a tornado came through it did a million dollars' worth of improvements! Another said of his small town, that the biggest business in town was a 600-pound beautician. Back then, besides supper, there wasn't much to focus on.

But, it's different in the world in which most of us live now. Focus is greatly needed today if we hope to have closure to our projects.

There Is Great Value in Focus

Focus aligns your greatest strengths with your highest objectives. Being free from lesser-value projects allows us to focus our greatest strengths (abilities) on the major task. Focusing centers all of your creative energies on the mission, whatever that mission or goal or objective is for you. Are you a businessperson, college student, athlete, teacher, entrepreneur, or senior citizen? Whatever season of life you are in now, focus will be your key! It is your best thoughts centering on your best objectives. Add good think time to this and you are heading straight toward your target!

Often, we become guilty of oversaturating our workforce with an overabundance of new projects or new products to account for. This is what always attaches another role to a good worker, who is also good at saying nothing about his or her already packed schedule. In the area of our church ministries, this has been so obvious for so many years, and yet it's still alive and well, often for the worse.

We have created an organization that has a lot going on, but rarely do we see any of it done to perfection. Our folks are so saturated and double- or triple-booked with projects, we actually have no one with time to become that specialist that all of us would like to be. If we would be honest with our bottom lines, we could see it. Our problem is in facing reality. We rarely if ever evaluate, so we become satisfied with less than the best. That's a sad day. Focus, concentrate, zoom in on taking one good hard look at your bottom line, and probably in your disgust you will make some changes. Focus does that. *Push yourself* to focus and see what could make it all better.

Focus Ensures Fewer Mistakes

Taking the time to focus and concentrate on the specifics ensures fewer mistakes. The details are what get you there, so focus there.

With less specifics to consider, more time can be spent on the essentials and the details it will take to make those essentials happen.

With over forty years in children's ministry, I have seen that it's the details that make the difference between a ho-hum event and one that is close to perfection. Whatever bears the greatest fruit must dominate my time. Focus helps me to decide that. Focus on achievement! *Push yourself* to make this word *focus* no longer an occasional good word to use but an everyday habit. That's who you are and what you do. It's that 20 percent of the project that is the most crucial of all.

Focus is also a good word for your everyday use. Some big projects can easily rev up focus because the goal is so clear. This word could make every day important and significant for you, your family, your business, or your ministry.

At one time our church was the second largest in the nation, with over 10,000 people showing up every Sunday. In the seventies and eighties, there were fewer "mega-sized" churches than we have today. Many times focus is what kept our children and teen ministries pushing ourselves to reach the youth of Chattanooga. I can remember seeing over seven thousand teens sitting in our auditorium, listening to a very clear Gospel message. What a thrill!

To do that, it took about two months of focus to cover all our bases. That's what the details are. We got our speaker in front of 15,000 public school students with a drug-alcohol message to help them and then invited them to our church on a Friday night. There the answer to the entire problem was wrapped up in a message about the Savior.

Focus is what set the strategy in place. The permissions, the scheduling, the advanced public address systems, the tickets for students, the preparation for the big night, and a myriad of other details is what made it turn out as a first-class event, exceeding our dreams. Focus on each step made sure that the next step was in place when needed.

We had neighborhood Bible clubs weekly that totaled a thousand teens each week. Focus took us there and kept us there. Casualness would never have helped to interest anyone to have a part. When you focus, you clearly define your own role as well as a multitude of roles. The *team* will be what takes you there, and that demands focus.

Focus Makes Better Use of Our Time

When I focus, it also allows me to see how much time is actually spent on the mission.

I have one life to live, and this is it. I must learn to *push myself!* I must achieve those most significant tasks that lie before me.

Here is an excellent thought from Brian Tracy in *Time Power*: "one of the keys to setting priorities and good time management is to get better and better doing more and more of the few things you do that make more of a difference than anything else. The better you are at what you do, the more you will get done in a shorter period of time."

John Maxwell, in *Thinking for a Change*, says this: "Focus your strengths, the things that make best use of your skills and God-given talents. What brings you the highest returns? Give 80 percent of your effort to the top 20 percent that is most important." What bears fruit?

Dr. Howard Hendricks of the Dallas Theological Seminary said, "If anything has kept me on track all these years, it's being skewered to this principle of central focus. There are many things I can do, but I have to narrow it down to the one thing I must do. The secret of concentration is elimination."

Another author wrote: "Devoting a little of yourself to every-thing means committing a great deal of yourself to nothing." Whoa, Nellie! I'm not sure I want to hear that, but some things that are hard to hear are the best to hear. Just a small statement such as this could be my wake-up call. *Push yourself* to a place where that is not said of you!

Programs, methods, and techniques will always need some changes and adjustments along the way. The objectives of your mission may stay the same for years to come, but the methods can change often. *Push yourself* to be willing to change, even if it was your bright idea at the beginning.

Focus Gives You an Honest Look at Reality

When you focus, you are evaluating whether the program or plan is actually helping to accomplish the mission. Your whole heart and soul must go into the mission. The passion or the drive inside is fed by the mission.

Focus brings us to consider the human and fiscal resources spent on programs. Often, our businesses or our churches spend their best and most resources on mediocre programs. Whatever bears the most fruit that resembles what we dreamed of all along needs to get our focus.

Whether we need to downsize to eliminate steps, roles, objectives, or time, we must be willing to *push ourselves* to that goal. Sometimes, eliminating is our answer. When leadership is allowed to focus on less, it allows more concentration on that which is critical to the whole. That's nothing revolutionary. Focus helps us to see the answer that lack of focus will pass right on by. How refreshing to see someone lead an unproductive project to get back on course!

That same leadership, now with more time to focus, should see more ideas and better options than ever before. You reorganize to come up with ten or twenty minds focusing on the project, instead of the two or three minds before. Anticipate super answers! *Push yourself* to that end.

Have we focused enough on the gigantic word called *focus*, or did you not get the point? Feel free to read this chapter again with greater focus. *Push yourself* to understand this good word as a lifestyle!

Key Thoughts to Remember/Action Tips

1. You will never have enough time to focus on everything, you must choose.
2. Pick one out and try it this week.
3. Focus on home, family, or a new skill. Counsel a young couple, help out a college student, or focus time on an elderly widow.
4. Eliminate the lesser essentials.
5. Remember the Pareto Principle of 80/20.
6. Train yourself to become a specialist in the goal you set.
7. By doing less, but the important less, we actually achieve more in results.
8. Assign a place and time and have the tools on hand that can eliminate time consumers and distractions when you are ready to focus.

10

Innovation Will Solve My Problems, Pushing Me Forward!

Preview...

The more you read, the more creative you become. When you read of a creative idea, your mind immediately applies it to the project on your mind. We innovate to raise an existing idea to fit our need. I like to say the two combinations of *reading* and *thinking* will continually make you creative.

I have had a large and exciting laboratory for learning more about creativity. As the director of the children and teen ministries in a very large church, the pressure was on. It was time to think and innovate.

Remember to use those short thought-provoking questions: What if I doubled it, shortened it, made it longer, brighter, more portable? Questions cause thinking. Thinking enlarges your options. Options bring better solutions.

*D*eveloping your own creativity is a long-term mind-set for those who will head the pack. It is not that the burden falls totally upon your shoulders, and everyone else just waits until that great idea drips from your lips. *Others* must be led to be a part of the process, whether that mind-set is in place or not. The business, school, or church *without* the *all-contributing team* will always be in for a long, slow-growth process.

Creativity can be as simple as taking an existing idea and questioning yourself: What if I doubled it, shortened it, or expanded the number involved? What if I did it every day, once a month? What if it was bigger, louder, brighter, or more portable? Questions bring the creativity for many people!

Good ideas come when you think. When you refuse to take time to think, nothing comes out. Thinking generates more thinking, and that's where the ideas come from. Becoming a good thinker is not complicated. It is a discipline that we can learn but demands self-discipline to set yourself up in a think time. I mentioned a think time in another chapter. This is the practice that changed my life for good!

Walt Disney said, "It's always fun to do the impossible." And he said, "Impossible dreams don't know they're impossible."

The people in your life impact your thinking. Find people who will stretch you. (Take them out to eat—I'm available almost any time!)

Thinking brings the impossible or at least the improbable ideas to a realistic possibility. That will *push you* for months to come.

The idea *generator* is the person we call creative. Jack Welch, a longtime CEO for GE, said, "That hero is the one with the ideas." But, without a team of *implementers*, every man comes to his level of incompetence.

Peter Drucker, a management guru, said, "Abandoning the obsolete, the irrelevant, or the program with promise that never materialized is the key to innovation."

Learning To Innovate

You will occasionally find that you come up with a new idea almost as if you are the first person in history to think of it. But, more often than not, your "new" idea was thought of hundreds of years ago. But that's all right. The think time brought that idea out, and with a bit of adjustment it could work like a new idea. Albert Einstein said, "Imagination is more important than knowledge."

Creativity is a thinking process where there are no boundaries to rapid thoughts, such as in brainstorming. Let the thoughts flow, many of them. Later, you can weed out all the ideas until the best ones are left. From ten ideas, bring it down to five, then three, then choose the best one and go with it. If it falters, you still have three or four other ideas.

Sometimes you win, but sometimes the idea doesn't pan out. Sometimes you sink, and sometimes you swim. Even then, sinking will make you want to swim all the more!

One of the best books you can add to your reading library is John Maxwell's *Thinking for a Change*. It is a most excellent book that you will read over and over. Few books do I read multiple times, but this is one! On page 114, he states, "Seldom do I have an original idea. Often I take an idea that someone else gives me and raise it to a higher level. That has been my approach to creativity."

What an honest confession, and what great wisdom for us to grab onto early in life. That means that creativity is not just waiting for that lightning bolt to spell out an idea in words in the sky. We can look at existing materials or ideas or the techniques and see how to do them better or how to improvise for our particular ministry. It is exhilarating to gain a positive thought that seems good on the surface. It gives you that shot of energy to start!

Some Guidelines to Becoming Creative

1. **Learn the process of selecting several options.** For most projects you wish to begin, there are probably more options than the first one you think of. There is usually not just one answer to your problem. I have literally had hundreds of times when this happened over the years. Once you think of your first way to make it happen, there is probably a better one just around the corner. Put them all down, without final judgment, then go back and make your number one choice.

2. **Brainstorm all of your workers.** They have the ability to think too. Maybe they have never spent any time thinking about your project. Some know the process, some will grad-

ually catch on, but you will not know the quality of some to help you without giving them the opportunity. Brainstorming is a means of collecting thoughts, many thoughts on one subject. All of a sudden you now have a resource of multiple possibilities!

3. **Imagination is an absolutely wonderful word.** God has implanted all of us with the ability to imagine and to say "What if . . .?"—"What would happen if we did this?" The more you imagine, the closer you are coming to that best solution. Your role as the project manager is to spot that idea that feels good! See what will work. You will always have plenty of others who only see the problem.

   Don't be afraid to fail. Every failure should only make you better. Will you ever do that again? No. But it does lead you to evaluate the failure and to see the process that brought it about, which in turn will improve your thoughts for the solution. There are just too many variables or uncertainties for you to always be right the first time. Just the variable of people will cause many original directions to be changed or modified along the way.

4. **Always, always, evaluate your ministry.** One whole chapter of this book is dedicated to that process. Evaluation is a part of the creativity process as you search for the better way. Taking the time to evaluate will be a great investment to make on all your projects. You are anticipating finding a better, faster, less costly, more effective solution. I love to stop, evaluate, tweak, and move on! When I see how to fix it or improve my project, that *pushes me!*

Practice being creative until it becomes a habit for you to look at the same project, the methodology, the time involved in production, the cost, the options, and just wonder "what if." Are there new and better methods, new materials, shortcuts, less costly ways of get the same result?

While traveling, look at the billboards as each passes and evaluate them on the basis of which one grabs your attention first. Are the words phrased the best? In five seconds can you understand what they are selling? How would you make it better, brighter, better worded? It simply makes you think. You look at it, evaluate it, and improve it.

Coming up with options for any project is also being creative. Think of another way, which may open up a series of other ways. That's how it works. But without the effort to think, I become one of those persons who just goes through life saying, "I'm not good at that." As we would say back in the hills, "Phooey!" "Baloney!" is another good expression.

I carry with me a newspaper illustration from when Delta was in deep trouble. The CEO at that time was listing his options to get this huge airline out of the pits and back on solid ground. He listed each option and then the risk of going that way:

> **Wait and see.**
> Fuel prices could fall and Delta could get the pension relief it seeks from Congress, allowing the crisis to abate.
> **The Risk.**
> Fuel markets are unstable; the Transportation Department has been silent on the airline crisis and what Congress might do is uncertain.

As he continued, he listed six more scenarios:

> **Shed assets.** *The Risk.*
> **Get smaller.** *The Risk.*
> **Push the leverage button.** *The Risk.*
> **Squeeze labor.** *The Risk.*
> **Find a partner.** *The Risk.*
> **Drop the big one (bankruptcy).** *The Risk.*

That's the creative process. Let the ideas, the what-if thoughts, flow without questioning or debating at first. Find ten options, then take the time to evaluate each until the best two or three emerge.

When the business, the school, and the church have thinkers available, problems will still arise, but not for long! Someone there is going to think their way out of the difficulty. Someone has to do something about it or it may go on for a very long time. There's another place where you can learn to *push yourself!*

11

The Team Will Take Me There!

Preview...

It is a big question, but there is an answer. If you find yourself as the only one reading this book, you may also find yourself as the initiator of progress toward such a lofty goal. You may have to *push yourself* until others catch sight of what you see!

Just because there may be little organization now or a gross absence of training in the past, does not mean you could never achieve such results.

One of the most glaring evaluations of any worthwhile endeavor is to find that no one is actually in charge. I have often found that leadership sees the need but will go for months and even years without releasing authority to a worker who will get it going.

The team will take us to the reality of the dream. It could well be said of most organizations that the team will get us there or we probably will never arrive.

*W*ouldn't it be a great thing to be able to develop a number one team pursuing a number one dream? That sounds ideal. Anyone should welcome the opportunity of being on such a team and reaching for such a dream.

So, why should I be willing to settle for less? What will it take to have a team like that? It's a big question, but isn't a goal such as a number one team and a number one dream worthy of one good shot before your career is over?

You will need to describe in detail what the purpose of your team would be. Think in terms of your present goals, accomplishments so far, the right leaders who are in place, and the wrong ones who need to be rearranged or replaced. Whatever the ideal within your mind, that's what you shoot for, determined to settle for nothing less. You continuously *push yourself!*

Personally, my goal for our teachers and workers is to make them specialists in the place where they serve. Whatever the business may be, there is that ideal dream that keeps crossing your mind. Perhaps some of us have given that ideal up for a lesser substitution, concluding that because everyone is not as determined as I am, it's just hopeless. Instead of throwing in the towel, throw the towel so far away that you can never find it again! Go after your biggest dream! Remember: you have one life to live, and this is it!

It is so depressing to give up on your dream. You still have many years to live and be effective. Day after day of settling for less than your dream can become a habit, until even the dream is hard to remember anymore. That's why I must learn how to *push myself!* The feeling of accomplishment is what makes every day worth the effort.

In your part of the project, you may find yourself as the only initiator to begin with, but that's usually where a dream begins. There always have to be those who head the pack or initiate the dream that others cannot yet see.

The commitment involves hard work and the will for long-term loyalty toward the goal. If it's within reach, if it's possible, the question is not how; the question is this: is there a team in place to take us there? The past has ended, but the future is as bright as your dream! C'mon, *push yourself!*

The questions like those above bring us to face that bottom line. And the recognition of reality is where we always start. *Push yourself* to find it.

There are three areas needed to help our team of workers:

1. The Right Leadership

Without leadership, the dream will at least be questionable. Leadership gives guidance. Leadership controls the decisions, the finances, the calendar, and the time commitment of the whole team. Leadership leads!

2. The Right Objectives

What are we trying to accomplish? If my biggest goal is to just get by until next week, that's not much of a goal. Those who will take you there must be able to see the goal line. It's discouraging when you're trying for a touchdown but can never see the end zone.

3. The Right Tools

Tools are what you use to get the job done. Your workers need whatever it takes. Tools are really incidental to the first two, but necessary.

Leadership is always the key. And may I suggest the right leadership. And may I add the right leadership in the right place or role.

Essentials for Developing a Number One Team!

- Cooperation is essential for the ideal team. A team with a common purpose, putting their gifts into the team effort, can achieve extraordinary feats. *Push yourself!*
- Combine your gifts with your passions and you'll come up with great combined talents and greater possibilities than ever before.
- Confidence is essential for a team to work together, to stay together, and to keep their focus on the goal. Confidence usually leads to achievement!

Goals for Developing a Number One Team!

1. The team is clear on the vision for the project.
2. The team understands the details (the steps it will take).

3. The team concept requires all accepting their role, and all in unity.
4. The team always submits to authority.
5. The team understands what the destination or the win is.
6. The team receives encouragement and recognition.
7. The team agrees to quality training.
8. The team is energized through helpful resources (tools).
9. The team celebrates together the goals achieved!

You cannot attain a number one dream with a number six team. The owner, boss, founder, or pastor is one; a team is many. Many, in unity, can pursue and attain a number one dream of any size!

You are only one person. One person always has his or her level of incompetence that will shut us down and cause a maintenance mind-set. We often fail to see the inadequacy of one person doing it all until we recognize that the project is stagnant. Gradually, very often unseen by one person, the project shuts down those who would gladly lend a hand because no hand was ever asked for.

There is great power in letting go. Delegating but still hanging on to all the details is not enough. You must progressively become a leader of leaders. The key is allowing others to assist.

You Do Your Strengths and Let Others Do Theirs

Upon reading about great leaders who led their companies to make a dramatic difference, I noted that they were almost all focused on using their extended staff. They were not Mr. Wonderfuls in all areas of management or expertise. They excelled where they were best and gathered others to fill the openings they left. In other words, they were not necessarily well-rounded super executives all rolled up in one person. They had strengths, and they had weaknesses. That's not bad; that is good leadership. They gathered around them others with strengths that ultimately made the boss look even better.

The initial person who gave birth to the dream may have been a one-man show for several years, but he knew or through his struggles learned that he could no longer swing it as the Lone Ranger. He not only needed a Tonto, he needed a good-sized posse to assist him. The sooner we understand that, the sooner growth and added success

89

begins. There will come other times when a five-man crew needs to expand to a ten-man crew or more as the *team* gains momentum and more success comes!

As your worker base grows, management realizes that more equals more. More trained workers on the team racks up the results at a faster pace.

A big question is this: are you willing to let go of the credit that perhaps always went to you alone? It's a big question. For me personally, that time came about six years ago when the technical skills of this day and time were what would launch our Master Clubs into the future years. These skills arrived through the computer age, which came and moved faster and faster by me until I was primarily a bystander, without the skills that the last two generations and my own children possess. I wasn't against these skills, but my mind was just so filled with ideas and dreams and goals that I convinced myself that we could just hire our weaknesses (which was me). And, in a sense, that is exactly what we did. Now, with extremely capable young men and women, we can move along at the speed that is normal for these days.

Was that an all right attitude for me to have? No, it was a mistake for the future of our ministry. The good part is that we were able to hire others to replace my incompetence in the technological age. Oh, I can still think and plan and dream with our staff, but it will no longer be me leading us into the years ahead. Yes, I can do the minimum on a computer, but I love to carry my legal pad and pen and still think well and dream well. But there came that day when I had to give up the credit and allow others to earn that right. They are doing far greater and will take us farther than I could have ever taken us. See their work on the web at masterclubs.org.

In almost every endeavor, if we expand our workforces, we expand our goals, complete all to-do lists, and increase our output and our influence, which all bring greater fulfillment. It often only takes one leader to release leadership roles to others. The team will take us there or it will probably never happen. You cannot attain a number one dream with a number six team. The details are what make the difference, and one person cannot cover all the bases. Learn quickly and cheerfully to release leadership to your team!

The Accountability Factor

You must hold workers accountable for the ministry they have agreed to do. Accountability is one of the most scriptural principles in God's Word, for yourself and for those you lead.

Accountability is simply your pastor helping you to stay right with God. Why would we allow Christian workers to continue a ministry by being less than faithful, less than loyal, less than consistent in whatever it takes to perform that ministry? We would not be good stewards for allowing our workers to go unchecked.

No, it's not the most pleasant task there is, but it does come with your territory. You do it in a kind, private, and right-spirited way, but you must do it!

Remind yourself often that accountability is a God-given mandate for those in leadership roles. God is going to bring up again that teacher's stewardship in the position given to them. It's at the place called the Judgment Seat of Christ.

Think of this: when I rebel against being held accountable for the work I am in, then that is *my* problem, not my superintendent's, foreman's, or boss's. I need to adjust my life to get back in line.

You talk about accountability—the Judgment Seat of Christ is big-time accountability. We will stand before Christ and be judged for even the thoughts of our life, not to mention the commissions and omissions of our life. That is accountability! It will also include my stewardship of my home, relationship with my wife and my children, and whatever ministry I have.

"Let us hear the conclusion of the whole matter: Fear God, and keep his commandments: for this is the whole duty of man. For God shall bring every work into judgment, with every secret thing, whether it be good, or whether it be evil".
—Ecclesiastes 12:13–14

"For it is written, As I live, saith the Lord, every knee shall bow to me, and every tongue shall confess to God. So then every one of us shall give account of himself to God".
—Romans 14:11–12

Consult With Your Pastor

Your pastor will give you guidelines as to the level of decisions you will make as a leader and what type of decisions should move on to his responsibility. Discuss these at length in order to do your role well. If you are an SS superintendent, discuss such areas as

1. The teacher who is always late.
2. The teacher who never or rarely visits.
3. The teacher who does not attend teacher's meeting.
4. Nonconformity to dress standards or other personal standards your pastor has put into place.
5. The critical-spirited teacher.

Your weekly or monthly teacher's list or personal activities should tell you a lot about your teachers. Allow these records to talk to you and reveal both the good and the bad. After all, that's why you keep them.

It would be wise and most helpful if your pastor would *publicly* explain the areas of accountability and give you the authority to hold teachers accountable. The pastor will then hold you accountable to your role. It's the proper and right chain of command. Every organization must have checks and balances.

So, rejoice! Stop looking the other way. Stop reading your records and then doing nothing about it. Perform your role as though the dear Lord is looking on, for He is.

In *The Carrot Principle*, Adrian Gostick and Chester Elton say, "Our data culled from a decade of research show that goal-setting, communication, trust, and accountability are the foundational building blocks of effective management." Sounds like our fundamentals for a number one team pursuing a number one dream!

12

Vision Keeps My Dreams In Sight!

Preview...

Wherever you want to go further, it will always take more to do so. The written vision clarifies the goal. A visionary sets goals to push himself out of the past.

Vision is anticipating growth. Vision is organizing for growth. Vision sets you up for the months and sometimes years ahead. For the Christian, our vision comes from God through His Word!

A visionary voluntarily stretches himself to a new level.

A visionary understands that questions lead to answers, and answers will get you to where you want to go.

*N*eed to *push yourself*? Vision will give you that reason for pushing! Vision is seeing into the future. With just a little *pushing of myself* I can become a visionary. If your responsibility lies in leading others, then venturing into seeing beyond today becomes your lot.

Someone must see the big picture. What will be the long-term effects of what we do today? The visionary has to continually *push himself* to see into the days, months, and years ahead. But that is the most exciting role to play! You have been chosen to be one of few who can dream dreams for the future of your project or business or ministry.

Pastor Andy Stanley states: "Vision is a clear mental picture of what *could be*, fueled by the conviction that it *should be*." How far can we go? How soon can we arrive? Who will it take to get us there? What should we look like two or three years from now? What is a greater goal than the last one we reached? What is that deep-down dream that you gave up on some years ago?

You're not dead yet, so if there's still life, see as significant a goal that you dreamed years earlier. I'm at seventy-two years, but I'm not dead yet—and neither is the fire that burns within! I plan to push myself until my wife says, "Honey, no one's listening any-more." What limits do I have? Only me, so I choose to *push myself!*

For my ministry, I must constantly ask myself questions. In the excellent book *The Laws of Lifetime Growth*, by Sullivan and Nomura, they state: "There is nothing more powerful than a question. The reason is that the mind can't ignore a question. It may choose not to answer, but the question will still be there, provoking new thoughts."

A visionary knows that it will take more to go further. He competes with himself and strives to improve himself in order to improve others and to reach the goal. He *pushes himself!*

A visionary makes his personal performance greater that any applause he may receive. He voluntarily stretches himself to a new level. Successes are only steps to a lifetime of successes, not a final dead-end destination.

A visionary understands that what others could contribute is great gain. Recognize the contributions from others because they will make up your vision team. You cannot go to that high goal alone. Your team will take you there. *Push yourself*, and they will learn to *push themselves* as well!

A visionary sees that the path to the goal is made of multiple steps, one leading to the other. It's the steady steps that take you there.

A visionary knows that the end result is much more significant than the written vision itself. We need both. The written vision clarifies the goal. The strategizing I put into the project assures me on paper that I can get there. But all of this, without someone working at it or striving toward the next step, stays in the dream stage forever.

A visionary strives to see the future because the future implants big-time purpose to each step toward the goal.

A visionary is careful, yet without fear. He knows that even from failing at some points will come some of his best innovative steps.

A visionary is not afraid to ask himself the hard questions and force himself to come up with the answer. *Push yourself!*

A visionary understands that questions lead to answers, and answers will get you to where you want to go. Don't avoid questions. Take much of your think time for questions. It's what gets the ideas flowing. You probably have not been to where you want to go before, so questions stretch you. The moon shots by NASA came from many years of staring into space by dreamers who asked question after question: Should we? Can we?

"Answers, on the other hand, are closed ended. You can know them and file them away and never think of them again. They don't require any further thought." This from the incredible book *The Laws of Lifetime Growth*.

I make my lists for one, two, and three years ahead:

1. How many new classes could I have in place?
2. What new classes would I target (primaries, juniors, handicapped)?
3. Which classes could be divided to make two, opening new teaching spots for assistant teachers?
4. What new goals could be challenging, yet realistic?
5. What facilities could be improved?
6. How much training could I finish in two years?

In my personal life:

1. How much better could my marriage be in two years? In what ways? (Your spouse can give you some ideas!)
2. What could I have thoroughly studied in the next two years?
3. How many books could I read in two years?

Key Short Thoughts on Being a Visionary

- A visionary *pushes himself* toward the future. Most questions and answers are future based.
- A visionary sees himself taking those steps that will get him there.
- A visionary learns to use time wisely because efficiency will get him there faster.
- A visionary sets future goals to help *push himself* out of the past. He strives for something better. He knows that striving will help him arrive.
- A visionary understands that it will take a team to see the vision fulfilled and will dedicate himself to the development of that team.

"Always make your learning greater than your experience.
Look at all of life as a school and every experience as a lesson,
and your learning will always be greater than your experience".
—Dan Sullivan and Catherine Nomura,
The Laws of Lifetime Growth

Initiating and Maintaining Your Vision

Your personal vision takes root when you begin to cast the vision to others. You are spelling out the route to this good endeavor. You are erecting the road signs that will keep every person heading to the same destination. They will gradually begin to see what you have already seen. You're convincing your workforce to follow!

When you begin to personally cast vision to others, it will require your high level of emotions and positive energy. Here's where the top level of passion comes through, if it's there. No, you are not trying to fool people, but it should be a most impressive presentation of all your values and dreams that fills your speech. People should feel and hear in your voice your overwhelming excitement for this project.

Casting and maintaining vision begins and continues with you. Be careful after the initial revelation of the goal is set. It fades easily. The greater goal can become the lesser goal by the addition of projects, programs, and responsibilities you add to your own daily agenda. If you put the vision out of sight and out of mind, it will be exaggerated by those who could eventually take you there. It's got to be what you think about, talk about, and have on your agenda day by day. A once-a-year review is just not enough to keep it in the forefront.

Vision Generates Energy

Vision enlarges what you are doing, where you are going, the effort needed, and at the same time energizes you to do your part. The Great Commission is vision from God. We don't have to dream up a vision for reaching the lost. We already know how God feels about it. And yet, God chooses to use a person (you) to work out the details.

Vision comes from God and is always perfect vision because He is the source and knows all. We must learn the heart of God for our own lives and for the work He has given to us. So, the question is always, are we doing what our dear Lord commanded us to do? Or, in reality, are we just ignoring the Great Commission and doing a lot of lesser things at our church? *Push yourself* to do the *main thing*!

Once you begin, vision gives you the energy and the intensity you will need to put in the long hours, if necessary. Vision will organize your priorities. It will excite you enough to prevent laziness, burnout, or frustration when the problems arise.

Vision Demands Focused Thinking

Here is a great idea: learn to have a think time. It will change your life and your leadership. It will give you confidence. It will make you a leader of leaders. *Push yourself* to be that kind of leader.

Find time alone, even if you have to hide from others and the phone. Now, take one aspect of your ministry to think through. For example, in your outreach, and in trying to fulfill the Great Commission, start asking yourself questions. How are we really doing?

Take a summary of your records with you. What do your records tell you? How many outreach calls were made last month? How many phone calls, cards, et cetera? What about contacting prospects for the second or third time? How many have our total workers contacted in the last six weeks? Any? If not, why not? Who is making contacts and who is not? What do you plan to do with teachers who never visit? What about visitors? Had any? Do first-time visitors come back? How many? How could we improve on this?

Do my teachers have all the brochures, follow-up cards, and discipleship tools to help them get the job done? Are there new geographical areas we have not covered? Do we have any prospecting days on the calendar to reach new areas? If not, when will we? When is the last time we had a good brainstorming session about our outreach area? *Push yourself* to put it on the calendar!

In other words, take one area and think it through thoroughly. What if . . .? Why not? How? When? Learn to ask yourself questions that cause thinking. Lay out your options. Have a legal pad ready for notes and ideas. Remember, God is the author of creativity, and He definitely wants you to reach people.

Vision Requires Something to Strive For

Goal setting is a very biblical pattern to begin. Set goals for departments or classes that are realistic but challenging. A goal too large is out of the range of average thinkers. They assume "We'll never make it," and so there is not enough energy and too little faith to go after it. Conversely, a goal that is too small will not generate enough enthusiasm to move your workers to action. They assume that we will just naturally reach the goal.

Always remember that whatever vision you see that God has cast already, He promises to be in on it! We must lead others toward that goal. We must lead other leaders to stay focused on the vision.

Vision Is Anticipating Growth

Vision allows us to see into the near future, seeing a bigger and better ministry than where we are now. Seeing by faith is anticipating reaching more children for Christ. As we dream our dreams, we also keep a tight watch on what we do today. Without the details done today, there will be no ministry tomorrow. There will be no growth and no expansion of the church. *Push yourself* for the attitude of *anticipation*!

Vision Is Organizing for Growth

Vision is also seeing what it will take in excellent tools and training to continue improving our workforce. We anticipate reaching more (growth); thus we organize ahead of time for reaching our goal.

Vision Sees the Important Details

Someone must see what it will take to get there. God has given some of us the privilege of the nitty-gritty and sometimes the down and dirty unseen details. Often, the only difference in the average and the great ministry is the sum total of the details. Never tire of the details. It is the only path that will lead to the ultimate goal. Vision demands *pushing yourself!*

Key Thoughts to Remember/Action Tips

1. We all need time to dream greater dreams—that's vision.
2. List an area of life: family, security, travel, kids' college. Then think future. See the big picture.
3. Write it down. It's your vision. It can be changed or modified along the way.
4. How far can we go? How soon can we arrive? Who will it take to help us? What should it look like in three years?
5. Remember the power of asking yourself questions–future-based questions.
6. What needs your personal improvement to get there?

a. _____
_____

b. _____
_____

c. _____
_____

13

Using Time Wisely
Stretches My Days!

Preview...

We have one life, and this is it! Think today. Think this week. Think the next step.

Time moves or slows for no man. As time moves I need to become better and more efficient in my abilities.

For our purpose, I choose to *push myself* to get more out of my limited days of life. It brings the important to the forefront. It helps me to recognize the top 20 percent of my to-do list as the wisest projects to spend my time and effort on.

*T*here are multiple books available for extended study on the matter of time. Many are in the excellent category. Your desk may not always be clean at the end of the day, as most would recommend. You may not use an official time schedule as many do, and most recommend. From reading the experts, we can taste various ways to improve our productivity. We can weave our own system that works for us.

Obviously, we can't stretch our twenty-four hour days into thirty-four hour days, but the idea here is to be more productive in the same work hours per day we are used to and to be more effective and accomplish more than ever before. We will also give some hints such as getting up an hour earlier each day to actually make an extra hour of progress. If you are strictly an eight-hour-a-day person, just that practice will make you a nine-hour-a-day person.

Most of us have heard someone suggest that we carry with us a 3 × 5 card on which we mark our time spent per day. Each project will need a time to begin and time to end. Every event that took your time that day is recorded. The telephone, unexpected five to ten minute breaks, lunch, and so on are all recorded. I must have tried fifteen times to account for my day. Discouragement would cause me to lose a week or two before trying again.

Once the truth hits home though, after a full day or two of recording, the reality brings a hard punch. Now, the urgency to get a hold of my time of life management gives me the motivation.

Our days can always be full, but of what? What is actually moving us closer to the goal? What is our actual 80/20 list of daily projects? From my recorded reality list, what needs to go to my not-to-do list? The big question now is, "Am I that committed?" Why not?

Dedicating Myself to the Day!

There is a beautiful saying that's been around for years for church folks: "Only one life, twill soon be past, only what's done for Christ will last." Knowing the dear Lord, that has perhaps moved me for all these years as much as any other motivational word. But also apart from the Christian incentive to serve the Lord, the thought is good for anyone. You have only one life—and this is it! We will never relive today again, and yet tomorrow is a brand-new day. We haven't lived tomorrow yet! We haven't made any mistakes tomorrow yet.

The preciousness of life, one day at a time, deserves serious thought about our achievements toward the missions of our lives. This should weigh heavy on the younger (starting out) achiever as well. It's not just the elderly who, after 85 percent of life is over, come to realize the urgency of each day. By that time, the elderly may face serious medical hindrances that will not allow the workload to be carried, even though the fire still burns within.

Oh, how many of us wish that someone could have marked our life with the sense of urgency back in our early twenties? One life, and this is it!

In John P. Kotter's book *A Sense of Urgency,* he reminds us to understand a true sense of urgency:

"When people have a true sense of urgency, they think that action on critical issues is needed *now*, not eventually, not when it fits easily into a schedule. *Now*, means making real progress every single day. *Critically important* means challenges that are central to success or survival, winning or losing."

Lay the past aside for now. Think today, think this week, think this step to my goal. Could I get up each morning of life and literally dedicate myself to the *mission* at hand, the dream that's still on the horizon, and get to work on the strategy (the steps) to that dream. Using time wisely, having all tools at arm's reach, and realizing that this is one whole day of my life going by, I decide to work steady, smart, and with my eye always on the goal. Attitude solves many of our achievement goals, but it can also be the very thing that wastes my time during the day. Time moves on and slows for no man. I simply must get better and better at what I do and also more efficient at getting it done! Therefore, I choose to *push myself!*

Dedicating Myself to the Task!

What is major for today? We must have that in focus. We must remind ourselves early in the day of the task at hand. It is to this end that we dedicate ourselves today. Remind yourself of the value of the steps you will take today and how much closer it takes you to the goal! Do some early morning self-talks. Pep yourself up. Plan a small award for yourself for today's accomplishments!

Get out your *original plan, your strategy* (the steps to the goal), and bring back that feeling of what it will be like when the project is complete! In my own life and the multiple projects over these forty years, I find it too easy to be distracted by lesser items that try to write themselves onto my to-do list. We can read from several authors to learn how to write a not-to-do list and fill it up to the brim. Some of us would say, "Sounds good, but I don't have five secretaries to do all the peripheral stuff." So we either find someone to delegate it to or simply put it on our couldn't-get-to list.

A choice still has to be made, and it's up to us to clear our slate for the major work at hand. If we don't, it may again be another day when the major becomes the minor and the minor becomes the major. Another day of life goes by with no step taken today toward the *mission*! We don't have enough days to toss the major aside for the minor. So we give ourselves this day for the *mission*! We choose to *push ourselves!*

In the book *If It Ain't Broke . . . Break It!*, Robert J. Kriegel quotes another, saying,

"An executive of a leading Western bank recently told me that members of management were coming to realize that their valued and loyal employees were burning out in the face of their corporation's high-stress culture. She said, Because of our *'gotta-say-yes'* work ethic, my staff overpromise and over commit. As a result, they also *under-perform*."

That's reality. That's what really happens when we do not make the choice to consciously commit to our major commitment. There's a penalty for getting caught off base. Because it's a small cost to pay sometimes, we fail to add up all the little costs until the bill is much higher than we ever intended. Most big things are an accumulation of many small things. It just may cost us more than we intended to pay and keep us longer than we intended to stay. It's similar to the credit card debts of millions today. It was so easy at the time, so small an amount, but now so overwhelmingly large.

Dedicating Ourselves to the Strategy That Leads Us to the Goal!

We have already spent a chapter on strategy. It is the planned steps to take you to the fulfillment of the dream or the *mission*. Remember, tactics are those in-battle, or daily, moves, adjustments, and changes made within the steps you have planned.

The value of such planning is worth all the time you need to finish your strategizing. It convinces you, on paper, that these steps will be the best and most efficient steps to the goal. It allows you to think through the scenarios that might arise before they show up. As far as you can see, nothing should arise that someone hasn't already faced on paper. The accidents, the calamities of life can ruin it all, but to your knowledge you are ready for the normal obstacles and have already faced them in your plans. Therefore, you are now ready to trust your planning and to follow the steps in your daily work activities.

We dedicate ourselves each day to the efficiency of the steps we take. We have put in our hours of think time, and now we work! Today, I dedicate myself to following the plan, quickly, efficiently, and professionally.

Twenty Books—All Declare the 80/20 Rule!

I counted at least twenty books that I have read that somewhere in their contents have mentioned the 80/20 rule of labeling the tasks at hand. Called the Pareto Principle, it's hard to explain though so consistent it cannot be ignored and should be embraced by those with a mission in mind!

The most comprehensive work done to show the accuracy of this concept is recorded in the book *The 80/20 Principle* by Richard Koch. You cannot but believe when you read this book. Let me briefly quote from this book to help us see the significance of this principle:

"In business, many examples of the 80/20 Principle have been validated. Twenty percent of products usually account for about 80 percent of the dollar sales value; so do 20 percent of customers. Twenty percent of products of customers usually also account for about 80 percent of an organization's profits.

In society, 20 percent of criminals account for 80 percent of the value of all crime. Twenty percent of motorists cause 80 percent of accidents. In the home, 20 percent of your carpets are likely to get 80 percent of the wear. Twenty percent of your clothes will be worn 80 percent of the time."

I would personally have to say true to each mention above. So, what we need to grasp here is how that applies to getting to our mission. This means that today only the top 20 percent of everything on our list is the most important to accomplishing the goal. Yes, there are some smaller details that will make up the other 80 percent of the total work, but unless the top 20 percent are worked on consistently, the other 80 percent won't be needed.

We need to be reminded of how this whole workload operates. What's big, what's little, what can definitely go on my not-to-do list? That's why I need to read from now until I die. I must get better at what I'm doing. What is it that I have committed myself to do that is really significant?

David Allen, an excellent writer, reminds us of managing our commitments. In his book *Getting Things Done*, he lists multiple ideas for handling our commitments. I would like to quote two of them:

"First of all, if it's on your mind, your mind isn't clear. Anything you consider unfinished in any way must be captured in a trusted system outside your mind, or what I call a collection bucket, that you know you'll come back to regularly and sort through.

Second, you must clarify exactly what your commitment is and decide what you have to do, if anything, to make progress toward fulfilling it."

This book, *Push Yourself!*, has taken a different approach, but is needed too. We are looking at twenty leadership values and the overriding theme of *pushing yourself* to use them all. It's *intentional motivation*. I purposefully choose to *push myself* to get more out of my limited days of life. If I live to be sixty-five years old, I will live approximately 24,000 days. Excluding my childhood, teen years, college days, and now into my career, a multitude of those days (even years) have already passed. It's not a morbid thought, but to face reality is good. It clears the air. It brings the important to the forefront! *There's your push!*

Key Thoughts to Remember/Action Tips

1. Begin by evaluating each day for a week (3 × 5 card). Don't make changes until after you face the reality of your week's findings.
2. Compare your normal weeks, including the average interruptions we all face, with your understanding of the Pareto Principle (80/20).
3. Decide what needs to go to your not-to-do list.
4. Make your list to review after. Do I have all tools handy? Work steady, smart, and with an eye on the goal.
5. Is there a more efficient way to do a daily one-hour job in half an hour? That gives me two and a half extra hours for this week alone.
6. Ask questions. What is major today? Dedicate your time to that end.
7. Do some self-talk. Lead your own pep rally. Remind yourself of the values of this day.

14

Increased Passion Moves Me!

Preview...

Passion, you will find, will help you to *push yourself* perhaps more than any other motivator throughout your lifetime.

It's what is on your heart all the time, perhaps already for years.

It's what you can do for the rest of your life and remain excited and self-motivated!

In the book *The Energy Bus*, Jon Gordon states, "Your positive energy and vision must be greater than anyone's negativity. Your confidence must be greater than everyone's doubt."

That's what passion brings to your table, and it is often relentless, above and beyond any setbacks.

Passion allows you to *push yourself* with a never-ending source of energy!

Definition

*P*assion is that inside drive that just doesn't go away. Failure or success, it keeps bringing you back with achievement on your mind. It is what I am willing to spend my life doing week in and week out. I know that because it is where the fulfillment comes from.

Passion is intense emotional excitement. It is strong love or affection. This word *intense* seems to capture the strength of strong passion. So it should be in our lives as we burn from within with a passion for movement, achievement, meaningful accomplishment, and the reaching of our highest goals. It's that great intensity that we are fully capable of having that can help us learn to *push ourselves!*

It's that ultimate goal, that top-level of accomplishment desired, that realm of fulfillment that you always have your eye fixed upon. It's that area of constant thought. It makes you stay up later or get up earlier just to think of a better way to achieve the goal!

The *Webster's New World Dictionary* defines passion and passionate as "suffering as of a martyr" and "the sufferings of Jesus." It is interesting to note that the dictionary uses the name of Jesus three times to describe this word. That sounds like the most logical example to us as Christians, as we would all immediately relate passion and passionate to the effort Christ gave for all!

In our day and time, we may think of an astronaut who has the nerve to sit himself atop the largest powder keg you could imagine and speed some 15,000 miles an hour or more away from this earth. There must be some passion somewhere. Or think of Bobby Bowden in football at over eighty years of age. I can remember seeing my pastor, Dr. Lee Roberson, at the age of ninety-four, being helped to and from the pulpit, still preaching on "be ye steadfast, unmovable, always abounding in the work of the Lord" (1 Corinthians 15:58). At ninety-four, the passion had yet to subside. It still moved him!

Have you and I exercised such fervor before for our passions? Am I so passionate about that dream I've had for many years that it would *push me* when I get down, encourage me when I falter, and drive me every day to finish the next step? What would it take for me to back off or let the fire of passion subside?

Passion Is Sacrifice

It takes concentration, time, and effort to arouse and keep the fire within ablaze. Sacrifice your mind from unproductive things. No, we are not saying that a kind of personal torture must accompany anyone who succeeds. But those we hear about, read about, and those who obviously have spent their lives in a worthwhile cause have also chosen to sacrifice some things for the sake of better things. Those things that arouse passion are definitely the better things.

You have heard that we all have as many minutes in a day and a week as the president of the United States. For some reason, that has never uplifted my spirits. But it is true that minutes count. Hours, days, weeks, and all of life is precious. You will never relive this day again. On the flip side, tomorrow is a brand-new day. We haven't made any mistakes tomorrow yet, so look up!

To sacrifice your mind, try setting it aside and not getting caught up with the thousands of voices trying to capture your attention. Favorite activities, outings, or sports can capture your mind and hold it hostage for long periods of time. The telephone can extend itself to hours upon hours per week. Let me stop here, lest we get too close to home and your attention begin to wander. Periodically, perhaps a good honest self-evaluation is proper. *Push yourself!*

A passion for your work will need a time slot in your mind to stay fresh, a time set to dream some more dreams and to envision how to reach those dreams. Remind yourself often of what your results may be, and your passion will increase. Failure to do so may see your passion decline.

Sacrifice is not bad; it is good. You are *pushing yourself!* You are taking control of where your mind spends its time, and you are focusing more time on the things that bring you closer to success. When sacrifice is understood and self-discipline used for a greater gain, passion will become more intense. It winds your clock!

Sacrifice Your Time and Effort

Anything worthy in life will take both time and effort. But, if it's to achieve your goal, then that is one of the best uses of time and effort.

If you are a teacher, a better lesson presentation will probably require better preparation (time and effort). If you want to be a better communicator than you are now, it will take more time and effort. Some who have lost their passion seem to shun improvement. If they teach second graders, for example, they haven't read a book on that age group in ten years. The passion is just not there for their personal fulfillment or for their students. *Push, push, push yourself* to read in order to improve! The pilot, mechanic, and computer programmer all must be passionate about the cutting edge of their careers!

Passion Welcomes Self-Discipline

In *Encore Effect,* Mark Sanborn states, "Passion is fuel that drives performance. But without discipline, passion is just loud talk and noise. Passionate people who lack discipline will end up in life exactly where they began." Personal discipline is so easy to talk about because we all know it's a must but hard to undertake for a lifetime. Those who have undertaken the effort to *push themselves* to a greater level of achievement than is the run of the mill are the ones we all read about. They have paid the price. They knew what the price was and have paid that price!

Passion Gives You Positive Energy for the Long Haul

In *The Energy Bus*, Jon Gordon states, "Your positive energy and vision must be greater than anyone's and everyone's negativity. Your confidence must be greater than everyone's doubt."

Even when you fail along the way, the passion doesn't subside. It pulls your emotions together to remember the goal that's still there on the inside. In his unique book *Jump Start Your Brain*, Doug Hall reminds us how to cope with the setbacks along the way. He says, "Recognize that when one of your ideas fails, it's not a reflection on 'you.' It's a reflection on it. Failure is part of the process of learning. Your best teachers are your mistakes." Doug Hall's follow-up book, *Jump Start Your Business Brain*, is even better!

We have heard about the school of hard-knocks, and most times we would hope to avoid attending that school for long. Our goal is to recognize the truth of the statements above, but at the same time learn quickly and thoroughly the lesson so as not to require the same teaching over and over.

Passion Will Soar Higher as You Become a Specialist

You are gifted. Then you rose to a higher level of gifts from your years of practice, training, and experiences. After years, you have honed those gifts to a much higher and more valuable level of use than ever before. Are you in the best place for the best results from your gifts and abilities? After forty years in ministry, I am convinced that some teachers should never teach. Some singers should only sing in the shower (can I hear an Amen!). Some who work with adults should work with teens or vice versa. Working to improve your gifts leads to becoming a specialist, and that's where you can be exceptional.

Winston Churchill said many motivating things and lived a highly motivated life. He was awarded the Nobel Prize in Literature in 1953 for his book *The Second World War*. He said, "There's a special moment in everyone's life, a moment for which that person was born. That special opportunity, when he seizes it, will fulfill his mission—a mission for which he is uniquely qualified. In that moment, he finds greatness. It is his finest hour." *Push yourself* to become great in your field!

One of the joys of life is in finding that perfect spot for the work of which you are most gifted. Why should I desire a week longer to spend the rest of my life in an area, while another area would be the absolute ideal for me and my abilities? Obviously, no one wants to quit his livelihood without the prospect of another. However, could I at least explore the options that may be out there now or in the near future. Would not your passion be greater in the very spot you wish you were in all the time? It seems like the best way to relight the passion! Everyone has a place where they add the most value. Are you in that perfect place? *Push yourself* to get there quickly!

Choose wisely, for your choices will hold you back or let you go. Indecisiveness will deplete the very energy you must have. Walk toward the goal carefully, thoughtfully, but with great faith! Always take stock of the consequences that sometimes we fail to count.

Tom Newberry, in his book *Success Is Not an Accident*, reminds us, "Americans have been misled into believing they will not be held accountable for their choices and that they will miraculously harvest something other than what they planted. I call this the Big Lie. This dangerously popular distortion promotes mediocrity and underachievement."

So, we are careful to watch for the pitfalls, but at the same time are ready to hoist our sails high to the strong winds and begin sailing in the direction of our great passion. What is it you enjoy talking about all the time? What's the subject you seem almost like an expert on? That will probably be close to your passionate area.

After forty years of virtually few skin-diving opportunities, I still find myself hoping the subject will come up for discussion. My ten years of extensive free diving (holding your breath) still leaves me passionate about the subject to this day. I could talk for an hour nonstop on the thrill, the adventure, and the close calls of that sport. Our passion drove us to be in a boat before sunrise, sitting over a fifty to seventy foot deep reef, waiting for the first ray of sunlight to hit the water. Passion led to the mental and physical training needed to succeed above the casual diver. C'mon, let me tell you about it!

So, what is it for you? There's one thing, above others, that *pushes you*. It energizes you. It winds your clock. It always leaves you feeling fulfilled. It's what you could do till you die. You are more passionate about the subject than any others you know. You wish someone would bring it up in conversation.

So, go after it. Shed whatever keeps you from where you want to be. Become a specialist there! What steps will it take? Lay them out and start on step one.

Passion Can Become Great Encouragement!

Teachers should be a constant source of encouragement. So should we all. Everyone needs encouragement. The confident person increases his chances to succeed. Encouragement lifts up, builds up, fires up all ages!

Passion Is Seen by Great Faith!

The gifts and calling of God are permanent and enduring. Romans 11:29 tells us, "For the gifts and calling of God are without repentance." In this verse "repentance" means irrevocable. Even if we have never done anything with the gifts and abilities given to us, even if we have failed over and over, God's gifts and calling are still resident within us.

Yes, even senior saints still have much potential left. Now, your skills are perfected skills and with much more good potential than when you first started!

In scripture, a lack of faith always bothered Jesus. Jesus never reproved his disciples for a lack of wealth or intelligence or talents, but He did for a lack of faith. Our faith needs to be big enough for our kids to see. Now you are training the next generation – yours. *There's your push!*

Key Thoughts to Remember/Action Tips

1. Keep feeding yourself wisdom, knowledge, and understanding about your passionate zone.
2. What will make you an expert in your great desire?
3. Commit your time, effort, money, and focus on the goal.
4. What would it take for me to back off from my dream?
5. If your dream is no closer than this date last year:

   a. Evaluate your original objective or goal.
   b. You may need to rewrite it or update your deadline.
   c. Think hard before downgrading your dream.
   d. Clarify again your next step and add your date to begin.

6. Anything worthy in life takes both time and effort.
7. For the Christian, a fervent prayer life about your passionate area will make the difference.
8. Remember the key quote from Mark Sanborn in *Encore Effect*: "Passion is fuel that drives performance. But without discipline, passion is just loud talk and noise. Passionate people who lack discipline will end up in life exactly where they began."

15

Reading Inspires Me, Motivates Me, And Pushes Me!

Preview...

Reading of others gives you their lessons learned. It can become a vicarious experience rich in knowledge for your own pathway.

You read of crossroads that you too will come to someday.

Hear of the reasoning of others who have forty years experience compared to your five years. You hear of their mistakes and misjudgments, which become a welcome shot across your bow.

Books teach me, advise me, and share with me my probabilities and even the pitfalls to avoid. That is what awaits me when I read!

*G*rowing up, I cared little for reading. Oh, that I could go back and reclaim those years. My little world meant more to me than the world of some author.

From our small town in the mountains, I could have written my own book about caves, bluffs, creeks, rivers, rabbit and squirrels, bass fishing, camping, and hiking. Perhaps that is not as exciting as our days of computer games and high-tech entertainment features, but for me it was totally fulfilling. Have you ever cornered a wild bobcat in a cave, tracked a deer in the snow, or shot a thousand BBs in one day? That was all in a day's play in the mountains. With my faithful dog, Fritz, Mom could never understand how a young boy could go off in the woods and not come home till supper time. And a country boy in the South definitely knows when it's supper time!

I know now that I missed a lot because of a lack of desire to read. At the age of twenty-nine and my entrance into college, my quest for reading picked up steam.

Reading is a way of life, a lifestyle, and a necessity. We must read to gain knowledge from others that have been that way before! Reading relates the profitable experiences of others, whether good or bad. We see their passion jumping off the pages to influence us. One must *push himself* to make reading an upmost priority.

Books Are Like a Good Sit-Down Interview

Imagine this, an author, quite often at the top of his field, has spent hundreds of hours in thought, sorting out his best thoughts just for you, and they are all in the book that you hold in your hand. I always enjoy reading the flyleaf of a new book. This tells me where the author has been and some of the impact he or she has had on others along the way. The author will give us his best thoughts. One could probably not get all he has selected as the best to give you if you sat in his presence for a week. It's the best lines, the best quotes, the best thoughts, the best conclusions, and the best options after years of experience!

If you are reading in the area of your own expertise, you will be confirmed for the same decisions you have made or you may see a warning shot across your bow. Either way, you win!

Books Remind the Reader of Older Ideas Too

My reference here is all our learning and exposures from the past. Our future work will someday be the past for others who follow. In the early seventies and eighties, I was there when our church grew by the thousands. I know what that took. My responsibilities included the full children and teenage ministries. We also started single and young married ministries for those who lived in Chattanooga. At that time every idea, every creative act was almost like something brand-new for me. Now, those ideas are considered "older" ideas. Yet, out of the "old" many still work today, while others need to be discarded or tweaked for today's plan. Old ideas are not all bad. I have had a multitude of old ideas. Some were good, some very good, and some I refuse to talk about.

But there were also hard lessons learned that brought wiser decisions for future ideas. Some of the older ideas are like principles in life; they still work and always will. For example, a saying I heard over forty years ago is one I have probably quoted to myself hundreds and hundreds of times: "The heights by great men reached and kept, were not attained by sudden flight. But they, while their companions slept, were toiling upwards in the night" author unknown. Sometimes a short thought from an author seems to stick and stay and may even help you for years to come. The Bible is full of lifelong principles we call key verses for life.

When you read from others you learn from their hard lessons learned, often from the school of hard knocks, which can help me to see the circumstances of the time and the decisions made so that I have the vicarious experience of seeing results without any cost to me! You read of bridges already crossed. You read of the reasoning behind the decisions. You read of honest confession of failures, which give you the experience without going through it! You read good ideas that, with a slight tweak, could greatly meet your need. I have read some books where I took two ideas from them and then trashed the books, never to read them again. But those two thoughts were worth the cost of the book.

One of the best parts of reading is to feel the passion the author has for the subject at hand. Passion, or the lack thereof, is so often the difference in *success*, *mediocrity*, or *failure*. I may be gifted enough to do that particular job, but passion will *push me* to do it with all my heart.

Personally, because of the years I have traveled this land only to see what teachers do not know, the passion has continued to heat within me to a boiling point of desire to help. I find thousands who are entrusted to teach children, teens, or adults the precious Word of God, and yet they have had zero hours of training in their last twenty years of teaching. A minority have studied on their own, but the vast majority never buy or read a book for help, never watch other good teachers and change for the better, and their churches have never provided training and have no intentions of doing so. Shame!

Shame! I believe their lack of passion has fueled mine to try and make a difference.

My passion has now shifted the thrust of my ministry of forty-two years to give the rest of my life to this desire to help our teachers. Two years ago I gave myself to this end. I give of myself, my thoughts, my time, my efforts, and my experiences, along with all the passion and compassion I can muster. My cry daily is for wisdom, knowledge, and understanding that I can expand rapidly in this arena alone. Only through the dear Lord can that thrust stay steadfast and focused. There is where I intend to *push myself* for the days ahead!

Reading is the resource I have each week. I search for the books of old with the great principles of teaching, the books now out of print but filled with the classic methods and techniques that will still work. I search for anything new that will work and for anything new that will increase my own ability to pass along to others. As I continue to drive the interstate highways, my list of ideas to think through, which I have always had at my side, are now centered on teaching. While I pray for wisdom and knowledge and understanding, I expect God to give it to me! To that end I am passionate.

So, why spend this time on a book called, *Push Yourself!*? When the thought of *pushing yourself* settles in, it brings to a reader the self-discipline needed. Teachers need to read in more areas than just methods and techniques. They need motivation, much motivation. Motivation gets some reading and thus provides more creativity for the classroom.

I love to read of Walt Disney. I feel the passion seeping out of each description given by those who served with this man of unusual creativity. He didn't keep it to himself, as his life was one of *pushing himself* and *pushing others!* He was so far above the others that, as a child, people laughed at him for putting faces and arms on flowers and for having a mouse or a duck to talk. One of his school teachers once called him to task for such artwork. He said, "Walt, flowers don't have faces and bodies." Walt replied, "Mine do!" I love that, and the world has loved it all for many years now.

Walt Disney's ideas, driven by his passion, built all of what we see and enjoy today. He is one of those exceptional people that we have had the privilege to have known. I keep a list of his accomplishments in a frame behind me as I type. I can't get enough of people like that. His influence, even since his death, still *pushes me!*

Disney said, "It seems to me shallow and arrogant for any man in these times to claim he is completely self-made, that he owes all his success to his own unaided efforts. Many hands and hearts and minds generally contribute to anyone's notable achievements." (Taken from Great Quotes From Great Leaders, compiled by Peggy Anderson)

That's why I love to read. Someone else has already been very close to where I am now. I would love to read how they took the next step, and sometimes it is the very next step about which I am so apprehensive. Teach me, advise me, share with me my probabilities and even the pitfalls to avoid. Talk to me! Show me the consequences before I get there, and I will forever be grateful. That is what awaits me when I become a reader.

Old ideas very often spark new or improved ideas. I welcome all that I can find.

Books Bring New Ideas to Me

The next author to read will bring a new perspective from a newer world of technology and materials never before available. The skills of today make the ideas of yesterday easier to accomplish. Materials are better, plans are surer, educated guesses are more educated than ever before, and specialists abound who are experts in all the parts of your project. History is behind us, technology is before us, and I can have access to both more than anyone who lived in the past, if I will only read!

For example, when I first started with children and teens there were few how-to books to offer guidance. Many of the Christian books were *My Ten Best Sermons*, but not on coming up with your objectives for children. I had the scriptural basis, but as the Lord demonstrated through His Word to the *followers* in the day He walked this earth, now you go and work out the details. So, it begins there, but the details are still our part.

So now, forty-two years later, I read a book such as *Next Generation Leader* or *The Seven Checkpoints* that are designed to teach leaders who and what they face in this current time. After all, some of the old still works, but we also need some of the new. Kids now face choices never dreamed of when I first started. Today brings problems that we never ever faced back then. All new is not bad; it just may be far more effective in this day. The Word of God is not the problem. We are the problem for not adjusting to meet the needs that have reared their ugly heads in today's culture.

It's the same understanding we must have for almost any job you apply for today. The computers and the web bring the worst of evil, but evil would still flourish without the computer. From the web, to the new technology, to our satellites, to the printed page, the message has the capacity to reach the world. I talked to a company yesterday that is so large and so up-to-date, they can now print an 800-page book in less than sixty seconds! Digital has changed the industry, and something later will change it again.

The printed page has the capacity to reach the world. In languages never put into print, it's easier than ever. The world awaits us all to use every new invention, new idea, or communication tool available to make any gigantic goal happen.

It is inspiring to me when I read of other individuals or other companies who are having success. It enlarges my dreams, my courage, and my passion. Old ideas, new ideas—I want them all. I get that when I read!

Try this: talk to the next book you bring home. Say, *"Push me, book, Push me!"*

Books Teach Me How to Think

The author is going to teach me how he thinks. I will learn why he went that direction, why he held off until later, or why he forged ahead at the crucial time. As mentioned before, I need wisdom, knowledge, and understanding. Personally, I receive the most from God's Word, but then others also help me with all three. The author shows me the wisdom of one decision and the folly of another, both made by the same person. I need that, and through their experiences without losing my money in the process.

For example, as you review an author's initial dream, his strategy to accomplish such a dream, and his in-battle maneuvers as he plans the steps, you can often see that it parallels the trail that lies ahead for you. He may have failed in some steps, but you can avoid the same because you read his story!

We are responsible for the wisdom of the past that has been recorded for us. Learn from history or be destined to repeat it. Our politicians could improve in this area. Books include history from the past, the lessons learned, and the great dreams for the future. Fill yourself with such wisdom, knowledge, and understanding.

Conclusion

Whether I read for pleasure, for education, or for additional tools of the trade, it comes through reading. I trust that you have always enjoyed a good book. If it started early for you, then you are probably way ahead of me.

Read often to improve your skills. *There's your push!*

Key Thoughts to Remember/Action Tips

1. The discipline to become a regular reader is yours alone.
2. Decide where you will spend the most time in reading:

   a. For pleasure.
   b. For knowledge.
   c. For training.
   d. For inspiration.
   e. How-to books.
   f. Travel, etc.

Don't forget whatever leads to your dream.

3. Ask God today and every day for wisdom, knowledge, and understanding (Proverbs 1–3).
4. Talk to the next book you bring home. Say, "*Push me*, book. *Push me!*"
5. Work out a schedule that fits your week. A chapter every two days or ten minutes after lunch or fifteen minutes here or there. Keep one book in the car for doctor's visits, traffic delays, et cetera.

16

Clarifying My Role
Settles My To-Do List!

Preview...

The lack of clarification is the root of lots of problems, even church problems. The act of assuming gets us all into problems, especially if our role includes leading others.

What type of scoreboard do you use? Professional ball teams have scoreboards that cost almost a million dollars. Companies report gains and losses. TV stations have their Nielsen Ratings. Sales companies record sales, quotas, and so on. Never fear your bottom line, for it's your true condition.

*D*oes everyone know for sure what to do? Most of us in leadership roles would immediately say, "Sure they do." But the real question is, do you know for sure that they know for sure?

I have had the privilege for thirty-five years to cross this country trying to train church teachers in practical principles of teaching. It is amazing to me that we can go for years and years assuming that our teachers are pretty good at this thing called *communication*. Yet, most leaders have never heard their teachers actually teach. "Well, she's a wonderful person, with a great family." So, with that we have somehow concluded that the same person has no need of improvement in the area of communicating a lesson.

124

For all these years, I have come to an unavoidable conclusion that most leaders have been assuming for a long time. When teaching the Bible is such a high priority in our churches, yet the training of those same teachers is totally absent, something is missing. I'm in some very large churches where teachers have never had training in thirty years. It's always on the back burner, always getting delayed, always planned for "someday."

The problem is twofold: (1) The average teacher just doesn't improve much on his or her own. Teachers are not against it; they just don't get around to it. They would come to training, but there is none. (2) The leaders or staff just assume all is okay because they don't really know. Perhaps they would not know how to train their teachers even if they scheduled it. But, whatever the reason, you have a workforce that does not know how to best do their jobs. That is unacceptable.

If someone asked you to describe a successful year for your work, what would you say? Or what goals did you reach this year? Or what made this year better than last year? Or what really matters in your job, your ministry, or the project set before you? What would you say? Most companies keep some kind of scoreboard. Perhaps our scoreboard should be as large and as up-to-date as what we see in the basketball game at the stadium downtown. There you have no doubt at all about who is winning, the score, the time to the hundredth of a second, or which quarter of the game they are in.

If scoring runs wins a baseball game or touchdowns wins in football, what would be a first quarter win in the project you have undertaken? Would we conclude that we are winning or losing? Are we right on target, behind, or way behind? Can you look at your results on any day of the week and be able to get a grasp on your progress? Does your workforce see what you see? Do they understand what the reason is when you apply pressure?

Whatever our win or victory or success is, it should move everyone in the project. Are those who can highly excel in this particular project spending their time in the spot where they will contribute their best? Are $100 an hour workers doing what they can do best? Where is the best use of your strength? Letting your time and energy be spent on less-productive areas is not wise, so we are probably losing.

Everyone is gifted with one or more gifts. Those gifts, our strongest points, if enhanced can reach perfection someday. So, the question again I must know is this: are my most gifted people where they can be at their best or do I have them sweeping the floor some place? That's not wise, so we lose.

In *An Enemy Called Average*, John L. Mason says, "Words without actions are the assassins of dreams." Time spent on less-productive projects is the assassin of your dreams and goals for that which you are responsible. The secret of any success we may have is based upon our best use of what we are best gifted for. Spend more time developing and enhancing the gifts and the abilities you have than in the areas where you are not so gifted.

Getting it done is determined by our daily agenda. For those workers who have a more limited time per week to give, getting it done will be those small amounts of time scattered throughout the week. But if we learn to use the 80/20 plan, as half the books in the bookstore refer to, great production could take place.

Clarification involves all of these areas to consider. Dedicate yourself to becoming absolutely excellent in what you do. Management of your time enables you to increase the value of your contribution.

In *Time Power*, Brian Tracy says, "Everything you accomplish depends on your ability to use your time to its best advantage. You can only increase your quality and quantity of your results by increasing your ability to use your time effectively." Keeping score reveals your condition. It puts it right out there where you can see and measure it and face reality.

Communicating thoroughly is your role, your duty, and your best move! What really matters? What is really worth the time and effort? If your workforce does not know what you know or what you see on the inside, they may have to figure it out or guess at it from their own perspectives. The last place they worked, the last boss they were under, or the last project that was similar may be their own perspective. That may be all they know. But that may not be what you want at all. That's why the word *clarify* is so significant!

We must all learn to be more specific when we attempt to communicate to our team members. "When you set a goal, challenge yourself with the words, *be more specific,*" states Jack Canfield, Mark Victor Hansen, and Les Hewitt in *The Power of Focus*. Sometime our goals are called *hard goals* or *big hairy audacious goals*, but whatever they are called, they are worth going after. If you are in the senior age level now, you might remember these big and tough goals from Mark Murphy's book *Hundred Percenters:*

> John F. Kennedy said to the nation: "Commit itself to achieving the goal, before this decade is out, of landing a man on the moon and returning him safely to the earth."

> Ronald Regan's goal demanded, "Mr. Gorbachev, tear down this wall."

> Winston Churchill's goal made clear that "Whatever the cost may be, we shall fight on the beaches, we shall fight on the landing grounds, we shall fight in the fields and in the street, we shall fight in the hills; we shall never surrender."

For ten years I worked at Pratt-Whitney Aircraft in research and development for the early space shots from Canaveral. The wins there in research for later production would amount to millions for the company and for NASA. The measurements and the quality control demanded the workforce be absolutely knowledgeable, without any reservation, as to the target. At times we could hold in one hand a rocket part that cost over $100,000, and you could ruin it in three seconds. The goal to be reached would not only demand perfection to fire the rocket but to keep the astronauts safe. The company's reputation, the crewmen aboard, and so much more demanded that every piece of work had a clarification attached. There were no unanswered questions.

Why can't my project be so clear? Why can't my workers understand without any doubt whatsoever? Why can't the teachers at my church be able to so clarify what God has to say that the student couldn't possibly miss it?

When a target is known by all and recognized by all, it will be obvious if we hit it or miss it. If we miss, by how far? If we hit it, can we do it again and again? Could your workers recognize a win even if you were not there? Generalities never give you clarity. We often stay in the generalities too long, leaving too many specifics for our workers to assume.

My years in the Marine Corps helped me to appreciate the word *clarity* too. There, you really did want to know for sure that you understood what your drill sergeant meant when he said something because he rarely said it twice. For one thing, you learned quickly to listen well. You learned exactly what a salute looked like, what level of shine your shoes should be, and how many minutes (to the second) you had to shave, shower, use the facilities, write home to Mother, and prepare your uniform for the 4:00 a.m. wake-up call. You learned exactly how a push-up is properly done, how to march, and how to stand at attention with your nose exactly six inches from the back of the neck of the marine in front of you. Your little notepad was held in front of your eyes at exactly five inches as you studied about the Corps.

The Marines, for me, *pushed me* to the point that I quickly learned to *push myself!* And that solved lots of problems before they arrived.

To avoid boring you with all the other specifics, understand that they were not trying to make your life miserable but to develop the discipline and clarity you desperately need in battle, which may be the only thing to keep you alive. When your instructor told you that the next crawl course you practice will have live rapid-fire bullets coming twenty inches above your head, that is exactly and precisely what he means. Raise your head to that level, and you die as one dumb dead person. But guess what? It was clear! We needed no other explanation.

So, when clarity has impacted me for that next project, that big goal, my to-do list should reflect the proper order of priority. And my not-to-do list should begin to grow (and isn't that a wonderful thought)! My list of items should now correspond with the strategy laid out to reach the goal as quickly as possible.

My goal for Master Clubs, a children's discipleship program for three-year-olds through grade six (masterclubs.org) has long been 100,000 children weekly in club. With God, there are no unrealistic goals. We may set unrealistic time frames, but with strong faith all dreams are within reach.

Leaders must initiate goals—or else no one is moving toward them. Clarification is a major essential.Because we are in leader roles, we must learn to ask ourselves the right questions, and sometimes very hard questions, to ensure that we have the clarity needed and that our workforce is just as clear. *Push yourself!*

We can use a baseball diamond to illustrate time for your company, your personal business, or your ministry. The goal of your endeavor is always to bring the project home. Home plate is where the score is registered. If you never score, you never win. You may hit a triple and go around three bases and yet still fall short of putting points on the board.

So the goal is that every team player tries to make it to first base. Without someone making it to first, there's no chance to go to second, third, and home. This goal is not to swing for a home run in one pitch, but to make it to first as soon as possible. Occasionally, a home run will boost everyone's morale.

In baseball, the first batter for your team is the one most likely to get on first base safely. Now, the possibility comes that the three or more hitters that follow will get a runner all the way to home base. Up goes your score! With one exception, everyone on the team needs to practice daily their hitting, running, fielding, throwing, catching, and strength building.

Even as professionals, practicing to improve never ends. There is one exception, the pitcher. The pitcher often looks anemic in all the categories except pitching. A pitcher works constantly on his strength—pitching. He may make $15 million dollars a year to pitch and will strike out nine out of ten times at bat.

So what's first base for you? Do your workers know? Bases for most of us are called *steps* to the goal or win! The whole team must have clarity about what wins games. The great home run only comes occasionally, and it often doesn't come when you need it most. The great goals come from hits, many of them.

In our world of business, projects, or to-do lists, are those every-day wins that keep on target and pay the bills. My auto repairman told me it's the smaller jobs, the $20 oil changes each day, that pay the rent and salaries, while the larger profit jobs bring in the greater income. He has clarified what scores for him. He has to have several good singles per day, while anticipating an occasional home run. To be honest, my repairman sometimes scores a series of home runs with just one of my bills.

Highly value the time given you today! Dedicate yourself to becoming excellent in what you do. Management of your time enables you to increase the value of your contribution.

Most organizations keep some kind of scoreboard:

> Ballgames: Huge scoreboards
> Companies: Report of gains and losses
> Schools: Individual scores, overall scores
> TV networks: Nielsen Ratings
> Solo jobs: Sales, quotas

Keeping score reveals your bottom line, your true condition. Never fear clarifying your condition.

A Key Essential—Celebration

When a team stops winning, far more than the team itself loses. The whole organization loses, the fans lose, the players lose, reputations slide, ticket sales drop, news reporting sours, and everybody looks for a fall guy to blame. The spirit within and without sinks to new lows.

Someone must watch for the victories and let them be known. Just as a loss becomes a loss to everyone, a win becomes a win for everyone. Spirits begin to rise when someone shouts, "We win!" Someone must be that point person who constantly watches for your victories. Someone must point to the win and draw all others to recognize it.

The church is not a ball team, but it must function as a similar team. A team should have multiple wins because of its multiple players, so spot them and lead the cheer. Celebrate your victories!

Celebrations Should Praise God!

Obviously, the church is God's work. He allows us to be a vessel and to be part of what He is doing. That's enough to celebrate right there! So when celebrating is done, give Him glory. Give Him thanks for allowing you to be in on it. Watch carefully for who gets the credit.

Celebrations Should Leave None Out

Someone must make sure that no ministries are left out of celebrations. It is wise to develop a celebrations calendar with specific times planned for celebrations. You must delegate time to celebrate. This is too easy to put off for another day. Some celebrations will come in a sudden moment of time. When that happens, praise the Lord immediately, whether your calendar says it's time to celebrate or not.

From the nursery to the senior saints, everyone appreciates being appreciated. Letters, e-mails, bulletin notices, testimony times in church, bulletin boards, and a public or private "Thank you" are all ideal. When the pastor says it from the pulpit, everyone can rejoice as a total team ministry. Look for ways to share what happened and to get the story out quickly. Lift the spirits as often as possible. Celebration brings glory to God and motivates workers to be a part of when it happens again!

You may find yourself in an atmosphere that has gone for long periods, even years, with little recognition. Although this may be gross negligence on a leader's part, it can change before the sun goes down.

"If you are going to hold employees accountable for their shortcomings, you must also hold them accountable for their achievements. It's the right thing to do. It's the fair thing to do".
—Adrian Gostick and Chester Elton, *The Carrot Principle*

Celebrations Raise Expectations for Future Goals!

Celebrations and praise raise the expectations of all workers to move on to the next step. It energizes you to do your part so the team will win again. Celebrating your wins is a great way to personalize the project. When I feel part of the goal, I then will see a greater necessity to do my part well as we all continue toward the goal.

Celebrate Whenever the Time Comes!
Praises can be daily and often. But never exaggerate your praise because it comes across less sincere than you think.

"I have yet to find a person who did not do better work and put forth greater effort under a spirit of approval than under a spirit of criticism. Encouragement is oxygen to the soul".
—John Maxwell, *Developing the Leader within You*

Everyone has the common desire to feel worthwhile. It motivates from the inside out, and the feeling pushes you to feel it again. Every personal achievement contributes to the goal and aids the team. In all probability, you still have a trophy or plaque or ribbon from years ago. It may be in a box in the basement, but you could find it if you needed it.

I can remember a great thrill as a young boy in the hills of Tennessee when I earned the highest award in Boy Scouts. My friend Bill and I were honored at a large gathering with the Eagle Award. I cherished that award. Our ball teams were symbolized by an eagle. So, I pulled the eagle off the badge and put it on a chain around my neck. Then a terrible thing happened. A girl blinked her eyes at me several times, and I gave up the chain and eagle, never to see them again. What a dumb move! I would love to have it even now to display in my office. That was fifty-eight years ago, and I still wish I had my award.

Badges made such an impact on me that the idea continued as forty years of my life was spent developing Master Clubs for children, which now has developed over 150 merit badges, plus ribbons, medals, and trophies. Children love them! Recognition is needed in most areas.

The personal award of fulfillment is one of the greatest awards that last for lifetime. Whatever gives you such fulfillment within, excel in what that is and the fulfillment continues to be greater. *There's your push!*

Key Thoughts to Remember/Action Tips

1. Have you clarified for yourself where your strengths lie?
2. List four ways to enhance your best strengths.
3. Remember: getting things done is determined by your daily agenda.
4. Align your to-do list with the use of the Pareto 80/20 Plan. You will do your best work on the highest priority projects!
5. See how many times this week you can remind yourself to use the phrase "be more specific".
6. If you are in charge of a small group, a department, or a larger work team, when is the last time you praised a worker or celebrated a team victory? If it's been a while, list below what you believe warrants a celebration:

a. _____
   _____

b. _____
   _____

c. _____
   _____

17

Faith Is My Supernatural Push!

Preview...

In everyday life we live with a great amount of trust or faith in ourselves, in coworkers, in the leadership over us, and in friends in various walks of life. We trust transportation, traffic signals, repairmen, and used car salesmen (that may be a stretch). The faith factor is a part of life.

However, there is a greater area of faith when we consider the spiritual realm that the Creator has offered to us. It brings power above and beyond our comprehension but is nonetheless available to the believer.

Faith will go beyond your ability to accomplish a goal within yourself or your own resources. So, that kind of potential is not natural, but supernatural. With our trust in the Lord, we have access to His power! It is certainly worth finding and exercising in real life.

Faith Corrects Our Self-Trusting Beliefs!

*F*aith in God goes beyond a one-time expression of your trust in Him for salvation. Faith is that continual trust that lasts a lifetime. That same faith can please Him, honor Him, and bring glory to God!

That same kind of faith will also bring the Lord's blessings upon your personal life. Only our self-limiting beliefs will hold us back from the highest dreams of life. We are to literally trust Him for life on earth and throughout eternity.

Let's examine how faith works in three areas:

1. Faith for Eternal Life
2. Faith for Living
3. Faith for Wisdom, Knowledge, and Understanding

We need it all, and we can have it all. It is the promise from the Creator of the universe. He is God Almighty, there is no other. One God, one Creator, one Savior, one heaven—all inclusive!

For there is one God; and there is none other but he.
—Mark 12:32

For whosoever shall call upon the name of the Lord shall be saved.
—Romans 10:13

Faith for Eternal Life

We exercise our faith in the Son of God because of His proof already to this entire world. He has no more burden of proving to finite man that He is infinite. His work from creation to redemption of sinful man is finished.

He died for me!

Made a Curse
for Us
Galatians 3:31

Gave Himself
for Us
Ephesians 5:2

To Be Sin
for Us
2 Corinthians 5:21

Gave Himself
for Our Sins
Galatians 1:4

Gave Himself
for Me
Galatians 2:20

The Cross reminds
us of what Jesus has
done to save us
from our sins!

His Own Self Bare
Our Sins
1 Peter 2:24

It was all Him
for us!

Christ Died for
Our Sins
1 Corinthians 15:3

Again, the cross reminds us of the promises we have from the tree of everlasting life!
The Cross Held the Only Savior of the World!

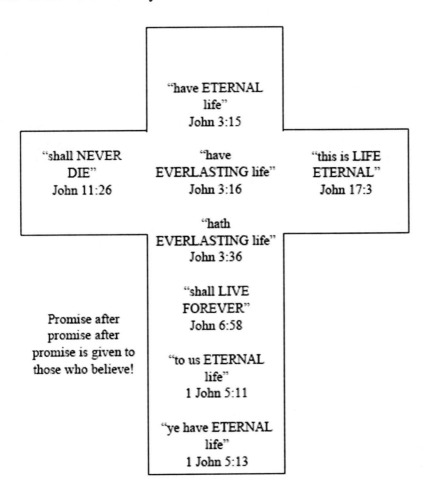

"That whosoever believeth in him (Jesus) should not perish but have eternal life."

John 3:15

IT'S JESUS!

"For God so loved the world, that he gave his only begotten Son, that whosoever believeth in him should not perish, but have everlasting life."

John 3:16

IT'S JESUS!

"For God sent not his Son into the world to condemn the world but that the world through him might be saved."

John 3:17

IT'S JESUS!

"He that believeth on him (Jesus) is not condemned …"

John 3:18a

IT'S JESUS!

"He that believeth on the Son hath everlasting life …"

John 3:36a

IT'S JESUS!

"For there is one God, and one mediator between God and man, the man Christ Jesus."

1 Timothy 2:5

IT'S JESUS!

"For he (God) hath made him (Jesus) to be sin for us ..."

2 Corinthians 5:21a

IT'S JESUS!

"Who gave himself for our sins, that he might deliver us from this present evil world..."

Galatians 1:4a

IT'S JESUS!

"Jesus saith unto him, I am the way, the truth, and the life; no man cometh unto the Father but by me!"

John 14:6

IT'S JESUS!

"For Christ also hath once suffered for sins, the just for the unjust, that he might bring us to God..."

1 Peter 3:18a

IT'S JESUS!

Make much of Jesus!

Let's take the story of the cross and see what happened on that day.

Two thousand years ago, on one special day, three crosses held three men. Two men were like the other people of the world. Each man made his personal decision on that day. These two men being crucified made opposite decisions. They made two very different choices on that day, and each choice carried results for all of eternity.

All the preceding information should establish the point that Christ the Son of God has already done the full work that covers the required payment for all of man's sin. The Father (God the Father) was satisfied with the Son and the payment in full of all men's sin. It is now every person's time to choose or reject the Son of God.

"For there is one God, and one mediator between God and men, the man Christ Jesus."
— 1 Timothy 2:5

"For he (God) hath made him (Jesus) to be sin for us, who knew no sin; that we might be made the righteousness of God in him".
— 2 Corinthians 5:21

It is essential that we receive the Savior before we die without Him! Without the Savior, we die *without* God, to go to a place *without* God, to be forever *without* God. The question every person on earth must face is that of *belief* or *unbelief.* Will a person be willing to die in unbelief and face eternity alone or settle his belief and receive the Savior?

God's example of belief and unbelief is vividly pictured in the Bible. Let's pick up the story again on that day of crucifixion.

The three crosses held two men who were dying because of their crimes in society. The law was punishing them for their crimes. They were thieves. But there was also a middle cross that held the Son of God. He (Jesus) was accused by the chief priests and elders and then sent to Pilate, the governor of the land: "Then said Pilate to the chief priests and to the people, I find no fault in this man", as found in Luke 23:4.

Pilate then sent Jesus to Herod to be tried again. Later, Pilate responds to Herod's trial: "No, nor yet Herod: for I sent you to him; and, lo, nothing worthy of death is done unto him" (Luke 23:15). Yet upon the response of the mob, they released Jesus to be crucified.

Therefore, on that day there were three crosses. Jesus came to earth for this purpose, not to die because of His sin but for the sin of the world.

The two thieves had one last moment to make their final choice of *belief* or *unbelief*. These men made opposite decisions. Their choice would last forever and determine their destiny. The full story is found in Luke 23:39–43

a. One Man Died *in* Sin

"I said therefore unto you that ye shall die in your sins: for if ye believe not that I am he, ye shall die in your sins" (John 8:24).

What happened when this man died "in his sins"? He died without God (the Savior) to go to a place without God (hell) to be forever without God (separated from God forever). Both men needed a Savior. But this man cursed the Son of God, and he died that way.

The Bible tells us in Romans 6:23 what we get from our sin: "For the wages of sin is death . . . ."

What I get for my sin is separation from God and heaven, forever. That's the place called hell.

b. One Man Died *for* Sin

The last part of Romans 6:23 brings a wonderful word to all of us: "But." "But the gift of God is eternal life through Jesus Christ our Lord." Jesus makes that big of a difference!

On that day of the three crosses, both thieves had one last opportunity. They hung close enough to see the Savior and to express their desire to Him.

The Bible says about the Savior: "Who his own self bare our sins in his own body . . . ." (1 Peter 2:24)

The Bible says: "For he (God) hath made him (Jesus) to be sin for us, who knew no sin; that we might be made the righteousness of God in him" (2 Corinthians 5:24).

c. One Man Died to Sin

 The third cross was another man who also needed the Savior. When he asked Jesus to remember him, he then believed and received the Savior! He died *to* his sin on that day! Here were his words: "And he said unto Jesus, Lord, remember me when thou comest into thy kingdom" (Luke 23:42).

This man was down to his last moment of time. Millions have died before they knew it was their last moment, having no time to cry out to God. The Bible says: "He that believeth on him (Jesus) is not condemned: but he that believeth not is condemned already, *because* he hath not believed in the name of the only begotten Son of God" (John 3:18).

Both thieves on the crosses had never believed. As the verse above reminds us, the unbeliever is already condemned, and it's because he has not believed, *"because* he hath not believed in the name of the only begotten Son of God."

Read the verse again below, inserting your name in each blank:

If (your name) believeth on him (Jesus) _____ is not condemned: but if_____believeth not _____ is condemned already, because_____hath not believed in the name of the only begotten Son of God.

When I believe, I receive!

In summary:

a. One Man Died *in Sin*
"I said therefore unto you that ye shall die in your sins: for *if ye believe not* that I am he, ye shall die *in your sins*" (John 8:24).

b. One Man Died *for Sin*
"Who his own self bare our sins in his own body . . ." (1 Peter 2:24).

c. One Man Died *to Sin*
"And he said unto Jesus, Lord, remember me when thou comest into thy kingdom" (Luke 23:47).

So, the story of the three crosses has both the conditions that describe every person on earth and the options of *belief* or *unbelief*. It also describes the one and only Savior of the world who offers eternal life when a person believes.

What is the person believing? You are believing in the death of Jesus Christ who shed His blood on your behalf, his burial, and his resurrection power over death.

Have you settled the question of *belief* or *unbelief*?

Faith for Living

It's our faith in who He is. It's our faith in what He can do. Faith is for living. In scripture, a lack of faith always bothered Jesus. Jesus never reproved his disciples for a lack of wealth, or intelligence, or talents, but he did for a lack of faith. Just as the act of faith brought into our life the dear Lord as Savior, so it continues as we trust Him for wisdom, knowledge, and understanding. This will be our third point about faith.

Let's examine briefly these two areas of faith in question here:

a. It's our faith in who He is!
He is God! "In the beginning God created the heaven and the earth" (Genesis 1:1). He is Creator!

"For every one that asketh receiveth; and he that seeketh findeth; and to him that knocketh it shall be opened," (Matthew 7:8). He answers our prayers! He is

> "Unchangeable . . ." (Numbers 23:19)
> "Unequaled . . ." (Isaiah 40:13–25)
> "Unsearchable . . ." (Romans 11:33–34)
> "Infinite . . ." (1 Kings 8:27)
> "Eternal . . ." (Isaiah 57:15)
> "All powerful . . ." (Jeremiah 32:17, 27)
> "Ever present . . ." (Psalm 139:7–12)
> "All knowing . . ." (1 John 3:20)
> "Foreknowledge . . ." (Isaiah 48:3, 5)
> "All wise . . ." (Acts 15:18)
> "Preserver . . ." (Psalm 121:3–8)

If we anticipate having our prayers answered, we understand there is one God who hears and has the power to do whatever He wishes to do. We have access to the Almighty God. Matthew 6:6 say, "But thou, when thou prayest, enter into thy closet, and when thou hast shut thy door, pray to thy Father which is in secret; and thy Father which seeth in secret shall reward thee openly."

If your prayer is honoring to God, within His will, and your life hides no hindrances to your prayers, God is instantly available. No man on earth forgives your sin. It is that relationship with the child of God and His acceptance of your prayer.

b. It's our faith in what He can do in and through me!
You have yet to see what the Spirit of God can do through you. From your daily routines through your full body of works within your lifetime, when God is in control the limits have no limits. We see evidence of God's acceptance of man's request throughout the scriptures. Bible scholars have noted thousands of promises laid out for the followers of

Christ. Many are conditional: "Ye are my friends *if* ye do whatsoever I command you."

> Abel's faith produced an offering for God. (Hebrews 11:4)
> Enoch's testimony was that he pleased God. (Hebrews 11:5)
> Noah's faith produced an ark (Hebrews. 11:7)
> God honored the faith of Moses and divided the Red Sea.

Living in our day and time, our faith should be big enough for our kids to see. Jesus said, in Mark 11:22, "have faith in God". Faith is above and beyond our ability to accomplish within ourselves or our own resources. If I can do it, then I need to do it myself. If I need it, I have the money to buy it, do so, and go on. I don't need faith for what I can see, but for what I can't see.

Faith for Wisdom, Knowledge, and Understanding

The book of Proverbs is a marvelous source for a lifetime of wisdom, knowledge, and understanding that comes from God. We would, of all people, have great loss if we failed to be ready to receive it from our great God.

Spend some time each day in this wonderful book. In Proverbs the key word is wisdom. This is the ability to live our lives wisely, or skillfully. This book teaches us how to relate to God, to others, and to government. The use of pithy (full of meaning and substance) thought, questions, and short stories all lean toward common sense. Each verse seems to condense fewer meaningful words into powerful short statements.

About 800 of Solomon's 3,000 proverbs are included in the book. The idea is to read at one sitting perhaps three or four verses and then spend your time pondering, thinking, comparing, and applying the wisdom to real life.

The Open Bible within the KJV is an excellent study system:

"Proverbs is one of the few biblical books that clearly spells out its purpose. The purpose statement in 1:2–6 is two-fold: (1) to impart moral discernment and discretion (1:3–5), and (2) to develop mental clarity and perception (1:2, 6) . . . Proverbs deals with the most fundamental skill of all: practical righteousness before God in every area of life."

"Wisdom" literally means skill in living.

Proverbs chapters 1–3 are where I return over and over to read a few verses, sometimes only one or two, and then stop to ponder, to consider, or as God has reminded us in many other verses, "Selah":

A wise man will hear, and will increase learning; and a man of understanding shall attain unto wise counsel.

The fear of the Lord is the beginning of knowledge: but fools despise wisdom and instruction.

Two of the most memorized verses of the Bible come from Proverbs 3:5–6:

Trust in the Lord with all thine heart; and lean not unto thine own understanding. In all thy ways acknowledge him, and he shall direct thy paths.

Notice the last sentence: when you first acknowledge the Lord, then He gives directions. That's the living part of faith, to "lean not unto thine own understanding." When I do that, "he shall direct thy paths."

The Word of God is not theoretical, but extremely practical for your everyday real life! Over and over you will find those great principles of wisdom. These don't come from a talented writer, but from the inspired instruction of God. The Bible is a study of wisdom given to man to fulfill the purposes of God. We see it on every page and find it illustrated throughout time and in the people who followed God.

> "Wisdom is the principal thing; therefore get wisdom: and with all thy getting get understanding" Proverbs 4:7

The Lord reminds us "therefore get wisdom" so we *can* have it. He says we can. As we get more and more wisdom, understanding will come.

The Bible is filled with words, phrases, and chapters that define and illustrate faith in real life. Hundreds of stories fill our Bible to instruct, demonstrate, and enlarge our faith in God. One step of faith after another will bring the most fulfilling life we could ever imagine!

When the spiritual vacuum has been filled in one's life is the greatest *push* of all!

Key Thoughts to Remember/Action Tips

1. If you have yet to settle the issue of salvation for yourself, consider reading from the Bible John 3.

2. _____

   As a believer, list at least one prayer request you have that is above and beyond your own ability or from your own resources. In other words, your prayer cannot be answered by yourself, but only if God answers: _____

   _____

3. Think of your largest goal or dream on your mind right now. If God moved to answer your prayer, would it increase the size of your dream? Increase your goal below if you know you could not fail.

   Original goal:_____

   _____

   Enlarged goal: _____

   _____

18

Goals Push Me Out of My Comfort Zone!

Preview...

Goals never set are rarely reached. Goals set without someone striving toward the goal are futile. The two go together or they go nowhere.

Goals give direction. Can you define it, put a number with it, or provide anything that will clarify the end result?

Goals demand good thinking. Goals give you a target to shoot for. Goals get the striving going! Goals generate the desire to go after them. Goals also demand a deadline.

*A*uthor and international speaker Brian Tracy states: "Your ability to set goals is the master skill of success." Brian Tracy is one of the top ten motivational speakers in the world. When a man of this caliber speaks, I'm listening.

Yet, in businesses worldwide and in church ministries, which has been God's choice for me, we are very poor at setting goals. Oh, we may talk about our goals, but in reality there is no plan for actually achieving such goals. Furthermore, no one is found striving toward the goal. No striving brings no expectation of achieving the goal.

Back in the mountains you rarely saw a goal written or talked about for the months or years ahead. Oh, they had aspirations and dreams like everyone else, but in my neck of the woods it was a bit more casual. For our family, the big calendar days were filled with hog rendering, sugar-cane squeezin's (molasses), blackberry pickin's, and turkey shoots.

Dad could make things so simple. You get up one morning, and after a huge breakfast, Dad would simply say, "Boy, we're plantin' 'maters and okra today." Then came those motivating instructions, "Boy, let's git er' done!" That's all that was needed. The striving began immediately.

Webster's defines *strive* in this way: "To make great efforts; try very hard; to struggle; contend; to fight!" Those are all good words to describe someone heading somewhere. Goals cannot be stated sincerely with a "someday" added to the end.

Goals Give Direction!

What are you shooting for? There's little reason to set a goal if you would never know when or if you hit it. Goals need to get above generalities and into the specifics. Specifically, tell me what you hope to achieve? Can you define it? Put a number with it? Do you have anything that will clarify the end result? That's direction. That's my target. And obviously I will know if I hit it or not!

There's nothing wrong with extending a goal, but there's a whole lot wrong with never needing an extension of time because I'm still at square one. Occasionally check your pulse to see why there is no movement toward the goal. Lack of faith pushes no one, while much faith pushes everyone.

From the book *Goals!* By Brian Tracy comes a great way to check our pulse.

The oil billionaire H. L. Hunt said that success requires two things: "First, you must know exactly what you want. Most people never make this decision. Second, you must determine the price that you will have to pay to achieve it and then get busy paying that price." Reading that makes me want to *push myself!*

Goals help me to keep close watch on what I do today. Without the details done today that are another step toward my goal, progress will not happen tomorrow. Thus, no growth and no expansion of the project is ahead.

Direction is essential to ever feel the exhilaration of achievement. Reaching the goal is achievement. It becomes very fulfilling and is generating the next level of energy you will need to exceed the goal you just met. Reaching that goal builds momentum for the next goal. I need that to help *push myself!*

Others, who you must have to get you there, cannot see what you see at first. Most others have not dreamed your dream. When you break it down into steps, they can see the next step. Each step becomes the next goal, all celebrated as that step is reached. Your eyes are still fixed on the finish line, but everyone else is still on the first mile. You will cast your vision and gradually count the steps as your team takes you there. Making each step with great purpose is enough to keep your team striving. Rejoice, you're getting closer each week!

Goals Demand Preplanning!

Strategy is your preplanning for reaching your goal. This early part of your workload is essential to the success of each step to follow. I cannot shorten this process, and I should not want to. If I fully intend to reach my goal, then I must fully intend to plan well.

But don't miss the joy in the anticipation of reaching that goal. Just the anticipation keeps you and your workers striving with the details. That's good. That *pushes you!*

When your preplanning is done, you are well on your way to reaching that goal. It solves problems, crosses bridges before you get there, and gives you the confidence needed to keep taking steps.

Goals Demand Good Thinking!

Someone said, "I try not to think; it hurts my head." My son has a Three Stooges T-shirt with a large face of Curly, his favorite. Curly looks like he's thinking, but at the top the words say "I try to think" while at the bottom it reads "but nothing happens." That's humorous in the world of these characters, but sad in the real world. In reality, thinking clears my head. For when I take the time to think it through

I am helping myself, ensuring a higher probability of success, and seeing potential potholes ahead in the road.

Thinking is not discouraging, but highly encouraging. We can't wait for this time to happen. It's that attitude of anticipation again. We anticipate a better answer than we presently have. Thinking gives us the satisfaction that we have done our homework. We're ready to proceed. We're ready to begin the push. There will always be some tweaking going on, but we are ready for the big push!

In my opinion, one of the best books produced by John Maxwell (and there are many) is the one titled *Thinking for a Change*. You need this book. In it, he says, "Positive expectations bring a positive attitude. They produce excitement, convictions, desire, confidence, and energy—all characteristics that help a person to achieve success. If you would like to possess these qualities in greater abundance, then raise your expectations."

Goals Give You a Target to Shoot At!

Wild shots into the air never seem to hit anything. We need something to aim at, something definite to hit. And when we hit it, we want to know so. Specific well-defined goals do that for us.

At about the age of nine, Dad gave me my first hunting rifle. It was a single-shot .22 rifle, just powerful enough for a rabbit or squirrel. Our six beagles jumped a rabbit, and about fifteen minutes later, they chased him back to the same spot. Rabbits always run dogs in a huge circle and return within a few feet of where they were jumped. Dad told me where to stand as the barking came closer and closer. Unbelievably, and I'll never ever forget, the rabbit came within fifteen feet of me, sat down like a little trained dog, and looked at me. Under his breath, Dad whispered, "Shoot. Shoot." I aimed and aimed and aimed and finally pulled the trigger. I missed him by two feet.

I had the target, a clear shot, and a brand-new rifle, but I totally missed the target. I'm sure you have greater targets than rabbits. In the goals of life or business, can we define the exact target? Generalized targets are never clear in the minds of everyone. Is there a victory if we hit the corner or the top half of the target? Does everyone know what a 100 percent victory is?

Without goals, you simply drift and flow on the currents of life.
With goals, you fly like an arrow, straight and true to your target.
—Brian Tracy, *Goals!*

Using goals is a great visual reminder of what the target is, and it's the goal for the whole team. Encourage them all as each step emerges closer to the target.

Lee Cockerell, in his book *Creating Magic*, says, "You have to go through the heart to get to the brain, and A.R.E. goes straight to the heart. And it feels so good that the brain thinks, 'I'll do that again next time.'" A.R.E. stands for appreciation, recognition, and encouragement. Mr. Cockerell used this approach throughout the World of Disney.

The goal that is set must reach that personal feeling of the team who will go after the goal. Seek to make your goals strike home. It has to cross that feeling line with those involved.

Legendary Notre Dame football coach Knute Rockne said, An automobile goes nowhere efficiently unless it has a quick, hot spark to ignite things, to set the cogs of the machine in motion. So, I try to make every player on my team feel he's the spark keeping our machine in motion. On him depends our successes. (Taken from *Great Quotes from Great Leaders,* compiled by Peggy Anderson).

Goals Get the Striving Going!

It's much too easy to slip into a comfortable position than to keep the push on. In all businesses and even in the ministry of trying to serve the Lord there are tendencies to slack off. When slack comes, the striving ceases, and the goal declines. It's also easy to justify your feelings. Instead, *push yourself!*

After forty years in the children and youth ministries, I now fight even harder to *push myself.* I have great memories, but those are in the past. It's always fulfilling to revisit them (the good ones), but it's today that counts. I can remember seeing a thousand teens a week in Bible clubs, over fifteen hundred teens at an activity, and seven thousand high school teens in our church auditorium. I can recall the small details of our mission trips and the lives that were changed forever, but that was yesteryear. What *pushes me* today? Why do I still show up for work?

While my mind continues to function "somewhat," I can't ease up on the push. Today, I learned of an operation on my heel that will have me on crutches for two weeks afterward. I want to die with my boots on, not wearing a pair of soft bedroom slippers. Life itself *pushes me!*

Here's a super line from H. Dale Burke's *Less Is More Leadership*: "Keep your dreams more exciting than your memories. When your memories are more exciting than your dreams, you've begun to die."

Goals come from someone's vision. "Dissatisfaction is not the absence of things but the absence of vision." What a great thought from John L. Mason's inspirational and motivational book *An Enemy Called Average*. Please, never settle for average. You don't have to. No one is making you. *Push yourself!* Push yourself away from the wet blankets of this world. Run from them and lock your doors when you see them coming.

When your goal is set to be challenging, yet very realistic for everyone, the energy and enthusiasm continue to mount. High goals push you. I need to be pushed. *Push yourself!*

In his classic book *The Daily Drucker*, management guru Peter Drucker says, "Performance is not hitting the bulls-eye with every shot—that is a circus act." He considers the performance of a worker "the constant ability to produce results over prolonged periods of time and in a variety of assignments. A performance must include mistakes."

That's refreshing! For a high and lofty achievement, your workers will sometimes take the next step and sometimes falter. The faltering is not the stopping point; it is the learning point! That failure may be the best training for the larger steps yet to come. The attitude of the one who heads the pack is crucial. Sometimes, and with some more often, you will need to come alongside, help them back on their feet, point to where the next step is, brush them off, and with your words of encouragement their fire is ignited again.

The early missionary William Carey said, "I can plod. That is my only genius. I can persevere in any definite pursuit. To this I owe everything." You and I too can plod. Plodding is striving, always toward the goal!

Leadership is constantly striving toward the goal. Others need to see your efforts. They can strive too; they just need someone to lead them. That's your role. *Push yourself!*

Your workforce will be the ones to get you to the goal. Now you have several or many striving toward the goal. You are not the Lone Ranger. You are one; a team is many. Many do more steps faster. *Push yourself* and you'll see others learning how to *push themselves!*

Words like *striving* and *effort* are good words for life. In *Wooden on Leadership*, the great basketball coach John Wooden says, "There is a standard higher than merely winning the race. Effort is the ultimate measure of your success."

Goals Generate the Desire to Go After Them!

Remember somewhere along the way feeling down in the dumps, stagnant, unproductive, a failure? It was probably not from a lack of ability or circumstances beyond your control. We just can't be a glowing testimony of perfection all the time. But despite our down times, life gives us another try at it, sometimes over and over.

Working alongside Dr. Lee Roberson and his absolutely wonderful assistant pastor for thirty-seven years, Dr. J. R. Faulkner, I learned to strive, to *push myself!* The loyalty of Dr. Faulkner constantly pushed him to accomplish all the goals set before him. He was a master of organization and motivation for the entire team that stood behind the leadership of that church. It was this leadership of those already striving that stirred the fires within all of the rest of us. It was very catching.

Goals *met* always push you to see greater goals met. It's like the adrenalin that gives the ballplayer that blast of second wind of energy to make another play. For years and years the goals you set and the steps you complete continue to give you that push to climb that next hill or jump the next hurdle. The absence of goals is often the absence of achievement.

The very act of setting a greater goal makes your day worth living. Daily purpose is greater when striving for that next goal. It is the cause for staying up later or getting up earlier. It is the internal drive that pushes me. For a Christian, the highest incentive of all is to bring glory to God. Therefore, when the goal will bring that glory, all the striving necessary is no longer a chore but the highest of privileges.

At the age of seventy-two, I have no desire to stop striving. It's understood that my effectiveness can begin to lessen with age, but that's because of physical or mental deterioration, not from a lack of heart. After all, the heart contains the real issues of life. Purpose, fulfillment, and accomplishment are all fueled from within. Then life is worth the living and worth all the effort given. I can't wait to get up tomorrow morning because it's another day of my personal life and another day to *push myself!*

Goals Deliberately Push You!

Think of next week without goals. What do you plan to do? A day without goals and reasons for living is surely a dull day at best and a lost day of life at worst. We need our goals to push us higher.

"The joy is in the journey of pushing yourself to the outward limit of your ability and teaching your organization to do the same".
—John Wooden, *Wooden On Leadership*

Notice the words John Wooden used: "The joy is in the journey of pushing yourself!" For Mr. Wooden it came in the form of leadership to the young college men he coached in one of the most successful careers in college basketball. But ball was not the greatest thrill for him. Read his book and you'll find his joy came also from leading men in how to succeed, how to live with purpose, how to strive with the greatest of effort, and how to excel in any endeavor of life, not just in ball. The entire school of UCLA benefited then and is still pushing the ideals of this great man. He had learned early on to *push himself!*

Goals deliberately push you. That's one of the great values in setting goals. There's the target; shoot for it! Measure your success at the end of the day. Review your step for tomorrow's day of striving. Take time along the way to celebrate your wins. Each step is a win or a victory because you are closer than ever before. The intensity and energy seems to come easier the closer you get. A week ago you were back there, today you are here, and tomorrow you are there. Your times of celebration can be almost daily, certainly weekly. The confidence builds with each step. The very act of setting goals and celebrating each step reached is what *pushes you!*

Goals Must Have a Deadline!

Do you recall perhaps talking to longtime friends and finding them still talking about longtime dreams, but they are no closer now than years before? In fact, I have caught myself doing the same for long ago dreams. The dream is either nothing more than a wish or it's just not big enough to generate effort (mine). Goals, set in stone, or on paper, now loom before me for others to see. It's like a question asked with no answer given. It just won't go away until the answer clears it in your mind.

H. Dale Burke, in his book *Less Is More Leadership*, states: "Focus on goals that, if accomplished, will make a significant difference in the growth or quality of the ministry. Many leaders devote most of their energy toward goals that are heavy on maintenance and light on mission." That's a great reminder for us as we evaluate the goal that was set forth. The "heavy on maintenance" type of goal can suck up our energy and nearly evaporate any enthusiasm for setting higher goals.

Set the goal but leave out the deadline and the pressure's off. Without deadlines, our goals are no more than words on a paper, desires without initiative, or dreams with too little energy to reach them. However, deadlines change all of the above. Deadlines are a sign that you are *pushing yourself!*

A goal without a deadline is like a smokescreen. No one can see through to the other side. Will it take six days, six weeks, six months, or six years? Who knows? It makes you wonder too, who cares? If you have the drive that says *push yourself* your goals will have a deadline.

In our Master Club program to children, we have the long-range goal of one hundred thousand children weekly in clubs, plus their leaders. Now, we come back to where we are today to see how far along we are. What this ministry has attained so far is very exciting, but what if we could double it?

For now, let's drop back and consider what it will take to reach the next ten thousand weekly. How many churches does that mean? How many in the next six months? How many in a year from now? How much promotion, contacts, and exposure is needed? What will make it happen? Deadlines push our entire staff. Deadlines cause striving, and striving is what will take us there.

We must push ourselves and our goals to become more than wishes. Wishes without effort will only happen because of others who do the striving for us. That rarely happens. The world is not waiting to rush to your aid. In reality, many of us are still waiting for our ships to come in or that unknown relative to pick our name from the family tree to lavish their fortune upon. May I suggest that we all stop waiting on the unknown answer to our dreams and learn how to *push ourselves!*

Goals Stabilize Any Weakness in Your Faith!

Let's face it, our faith or trust in our projects is sometimes lacking. When goals are set, they exercise my faith. When goals are out of sight or nonexistent, there's not much need for faith. Faith is stabilizing for all of us. Lack of faith generates little. Without faith in your boss or your fellow workers, who wants to continue? Lack of faith erodes your confidence, depletes your energy, and closes the curtain on your dreams.

Strong faith will carry you for a lifetime. As a Christian who believes Christ, my faith will carry me to an eternity in Heaven. It's not *my* faith that will make that happen, but faith in Him and His ability to do what He said He would do!

Faith is strong in moving one to action. Because you believe, you act. Because you act, progress is made. Because progress is made, goals are reached. When goals are reached, renewed energy will take you to the next goal.

Goals bring stability. You can see ahead of time where you intend to go. You can see those steps ahead and how each leads to the next. That's inspiring. That's stability. I can now convince myself that time and effort is a very worthwhile expenditure for me to make. So I *push myself!*

Even when an occasional failure shows up, the goal is still there. You can again refocus quickly on what you still see within reach. As Thomas Edison did with his thousands of failures, he never allowed them to even slow him down. Too often the very one who defeated you was yourself.

When we read of Edison as a young child, we see that he was dismissed from school at about the sixth grade as one who was not very smart or teachable. His parents were encouraged not to spend any more money on "this child" and his education. Thomas Edison went on to patent 1,093 products at the US Patent Office. It is strongly estimated that at his death in 1931, one-sixth of the entire workforce in America was employed to make his inventions. Of course, he could have chosen to just give up and become a failure. Aren't we glad that he set a higher goal than that? He learned early on, even in the face of hundreds and hundreds of failures, that he must *push himself!*

The last of our four children was born with Down syndrome. It was not in our family history, but that one genetic defect (the child receives an extra chromosome) does a lot of damage. However, let me hasten to say that as a Christian family it wasn't really a defect at all. We believe without any doubt whatsoever that this was God's design, not a freak of nature. With this child, I believe we have set more goals than with our other three children, who are fully capable of setting their own goals now.

I want to regress for a moment to help you see that what looks like failure can be beautiful. What looks like no need for goals becomes one of the greatest incentives for goals. What looks like little achievement could take place can become high goals and high achievement. Therefore, I want to share with you what is in a printed brochure of our son's life. You may receive one or more brochures free of charge by contacting us.

Being in the hospital room at his birth, Paul certainly looked like one of the Thomas kids. The doctor and nurses, however, saw the tell-tale signs. They saw the simian crease across the palms, the fatty tissue on the neck, and that small difference in the eyes.

The blood work confirmed that our child had received an extra chromosome. There is no prevention, a regression pill, or a cure. About 1 in every 700 births is a Down syndrome child.

Is there life after Down Syndrome? Oh, there's the best of life, and that's the rest of the story! Paul is now twenty-eight. Let me share the joy of Paul in our home for these twenty-eight years. Let me encourage you. Let me show you the good side of Down syndrome.

Immediately upon the doctor's confirmation, my wife and I fully accepted this child, without reservation, without knowing future complications or handicaps, and without any regrets to this day. We believe without any doubt that God graced our family with Paul. We believe he is exactly how God planned for him to be. The benefit has been all ours, being given the privilege of parenting and loving this child.

There is a wrong view of Down syndrome. If our perception of such a birth is as a freak of nature or a "Mongoloid" child, as they were called years ago, then the goal might be to keep him at home in the back room. He could only be an embarrassment to our family. He couldn't possibly socialize. In fact, he would be better off if we put him away in some home, any home except ours. He will only be a bother, an inconvenience, and will surely cramp our lifestyle.

The selfishness of our world has taught us that.

There is a better view of Down syndrome. But there is another choice, another attitude, a better way! It is this: Accept him. Smother him with love. Take him where you go. Tell him how much you love him. Give him a chance! The child will return far more love than you can possibly give.

Paul's early years: Help was available for our child from six weeks of age in an infant-stimulation program. His schooling progressed from ages two to three to four and then to preschool through junior high school. Paul graduated from Milford High School in May of 2003 in a class of 400.

During Paul's school years: The school system has always been a good help to us and has welcomed Paul and other children with open arms. Students escorted Paul for inclusion in regular classes. Friends were everywhere. Walking down a hallway, it seemed as if every student we passed knew Paul and greeted him, often with a high-five hand slap. He was on the student council. He was voted captain of the junior varsity bowling team. Even with his limited abilities in these areas, he felt so welcome and a normal part of the growing-up process.

Paul received over $2,000 in cash gifts for graduation. Seven of his former teachers came to his graduation open house party. Several awards adorn his room.

After six years of steady effort, Paul has earned his third-degree black belt in karate and is still going. In his church program of Master Clubs, he earned thirty merit badges, representing four years of effort.

Something better than awards. Let me share with you the character of a Down's child. Personal character, the kind you wished your teens had, is rarely a strong feature in children today. In our society, children grow up under extreme peer pressure, the Hollywood lifestyles (as if that's normal), the devastating role models of MTV and even the parental modeling (the kind you see in a department store when a mom and four kids come in). Values are fading. "What's in it for me" overrides all else.

In a Down's child, his life seems to be so much more basic. The God-implanted values just seem to come out uncluttered by the selfishness of this world. We are much more proud of Paul's character within than with all of his achievements of medals, belts, badges, and honors.

How about a child who says, "I love you, Mom," fifteen to twenty-five times a day, every day? A child who loves hugs and kisses in what we call at our house the "family love circle." How about a child who colors and paints pictures just for you? A child who introduces himself and his parents to all he meets. A child who has a wonderful work ethic. A child who is willing to give most of his money to help us reach other children for the Lord.

Paul has had foot surgery, open-heart surgery, and a most serious spinal surgery. While wearing a large steel halo screwed into his skull for over a year, he still shook hands up and down the aisles of our church. Always positive, everything is always okay, even through pain.

If you were obese or had a large wart between your eyes, Paul would never see it. He will accept you just the way you are!

Today and tomorrow in Paul's life. Today, Paul continues to help the younger kids in karate classes, in Master Club at our church, in his Sunday school, and children's church.

Paul also works at The Arbors, a nursing/assisted living home. He loves elderly folks. He loves telling little ladies how pretty they are. Once at our church, a widow of ten years came into my wife's ladies class in tears. Janice asked her what was wrong. The lady replied, "Oh, it's Paul again." Thinking the worst, Janice pursued what he had said. The lady again replied, "Oh, he kissed me, and told me how pretty I was. I just realized that it's been ten years since someone said that to me."

How Down syndrome graces your home. I could have never planned a greater joy and blessing to my other children than for them to have a brother with Down syndrome. They are not ashamed of their little brother. He has taught us to say "I love you" and to become a family that expresses that love as often as possible.

After every meal, it's always Paul who reminds us, "Sarah, thank Mom for the meal. Bobby, thank Mom for the meal. Jimmy, thank Mom for the meal. Dad, thank Mom for the meal." At home it's "Thank Mom." At restaurants it's "Thank Dad." He never forgets, and so neither do we!

I'll stop there with some of the content in the brochure. With his birth, my wife and I were suddenly given a whole new set of goals. But what a wonderful experience. Even through operations and doctor's appointments, this young bundle of life has given us even greater drive from within to assist our beautiful child.

Of course, we could have aborted this fourth child. A doctor's wife the same week gave birth to a Down's child alongside ours. She refused to even take the child home. Put it away in some home, any home but hers. What an absurd, selfish thought. Abortion would have also aborted God's will for Paul and for our family. I don't have the right to take my child's life, and I do not have the right to forego parenting and loving and caring for this great gift of life.

The goals with Paul are constantly growing. How can we better care for him? What can he achieve greater in his life? He has learned to lead songs in our teacher training seminars. He travels extensively with me. He gives his testimony and last year had the opportunity to give his message (about 8–10 minutes) in four large settings, one of over 2,000 people. Could you do that? So the goals we help Paul to set and go after give his life stability too. He has purpose and direction, regardless of the circumstances of his birth. He's not under them; he is above them!

In one of Paul's messages, he says, "Down syndrome is not so bad. I can still think and dream and serve my Lord!" I love you, my son.

"The first important step in weathering failure is learning not to personalize it".
—John Maxwell, *Failing Forward*

With Paul, no one knows where the extra chromosome came from, the father or the mother. We believe it came from God. Therefore, to move on we can't place blame, for there is only great joy and no need to pity Paul or ourselves. It has only been the greatest blessing imaginable. Setting goals from six weeks of age in that first infant-stimulation program was a great help for us. That's what goals do. They get you back on your feet and moving in the direction of progress again.

My wife, Janice, has been with me for these forty-three years through the early struggles of putting *Master Clubs* in other churches. No one saw a need to do so. But no one saw what we saw on the inside. While struggling financially to keep our family afloat, we were told to get it out from under the church and finance the endeavor ourselves. This had us renting a warehouse and printing in the middle of the night. God still had us directing the children and teen ministries in one of the three largest churches in the nation. My wife was our entire shipping department. The whole ministry operated out of the trunk of our Pinto (remember that one?).

Janice alone kept me from throwing in the towel several times. She believed in me, and I really did believe in the mission. Failure was not an option.

I learned setting goals under the leadership of our church. Every week, fifty-two weeks a year, there were goals, goals, and more goals! I'm grateful for those years. To me, goals told me the project was worthy of energy, time, and learning from failures. Goals gave us all the stability that we were following a leader who knew where he was going. When we spent time on the details, it too assured us that we could get there. The strategy of planning our steps made the goal even more exciting. Year after year after year our goals were reached.

Goals Will Keep You in Focus!

An earlier chapter dealt with the great value of learning how to focus on any definite pursuit. Goals give you something to focus upon.

Distractions are too many and too often not to understand how to focus. But focus on what? Goals give you that target, that specific target. Learn early on to set, review, evaluate, and redefine goals as needed. Goals set you on the steps toward your dream. There's *your push!*

Key Thoughts to Remember/Action Tips

1. Are your goals past the generalities and into the specifics? What do you hope to achieve? What is your ultimate destination?
2. Reaching one goal builds momentum for another.
3. Remember the key quote by H. Dale Burke: "Keep your dreams more exciting than your memories. When your memories are more exciting than your dreams, you've begun to die."
4. Your goals need to be far above the average and far enough beyond your own ability that you must trust God for it.
5. Goals need a deadline to start and a progressive deadline as each step grows closer.

19

Refusing To Put The Lid On Pushes Me Above Ordinary!

Preview...

The negativism of this day and time, sometimes from our own family, is enough to make us pull a wet blanket (a lid) over us and give up on our dreams.

However, the option is still open to buck any tide and to stand alone if necessary, but never to quit.

Your potential to accomplish your dream can fire you up while others have allowed their fires to die.

Refuse to give up on life. No one is making you give up!

I am not someone else and never will be. I have all the capabilities of being myself to the highest level, the grandest of achievements, and a life rich with fulfillment! I will *push myself* to this goal.

*H*ave you ever felt as though someone just put the lid on your dream? There are a multitude of people or circumstances that can make us feel as though all is lost. It's not lost; it's just some non-achiever trying to justify his own lack of passion and to make himself more equal to you. Run from those who fill your day with downgrading remarks.

Constantly read of those who have refused to succumb to the negativism of this day. Fill your mind with the dreamers of today and of the past. Refuse to sit for hours watching today's sitcoms where writers put out scripts as fast as possible. All they need for a script is a fistful of one-liners: "You say something to deflate me, and I'll return the comment with something negative about you." It's rarely uplifting, encouraging, or a strengthening of your spirit. Can you see this "funny" lifestyle lived out on the tube for the next six years in a teenager's life? Something causes even bad habits to take root in young lives.

Dream some dreams. Confirm in your heart right now to be and live above the ordinary: "I refuse to put the lid on my dreams!"

We must learn early on not to let our dreams fade or lessen. Every bit of loss begins to erode your potential to reach that dream. Allowing my dream to fade in its intensity, I just may begin lowering the limits of my dream, which originally had no limits. At the birth of my dream, all heights were possible without fear of failure. If not careful, we will lower our limits in order to lower our possibilities of failure. We must *push ourselves!*

When dreams fade, passion fades. When possibilities are lowered, slowly, on the inside, that fire flickers. Others used to watch you burn when you talked about the dream. Now you would rather not bring it up. Something is not as bright as it used to be.

I loved the Boy Scouts as a young child. I loved the camping trips and the competitions of our skills. To this day, I'll never forget the thrill as an eleven-year-old boy winning my first event in fire making. With flint and steel, I had a blaze going within six seconds! Needless to say, it was that first spark that just happened to catch that did it. They taught us how to rekindle the fire that was all but dead. Give it your breath of life, so to speak. The fire is desperate for air. Just a few puffs of air and you see those black dead-looking coals rise to a flame again.

Maybe it's time for a fan the fire personal retreat—just you and your dream! Reach way down deep to find again that ember that used to be a roaring fire. Dream it again! Dreams also need that deadline in place. We cannot just dream and dream with little action. Where's the push? *Push yourself!*

In *The Question behind the Question*, John G. Miller says, "Long range vision and strategic planning are great tools, but we need to get some things done before lunch." That is a book that makes you think again and again.

As quoted in *Great Quotes from Great Leaders*, Dr. Martin Luther King said, "I have a dream that one day this nation will rise up and live out the true meaning of this creed: 'We hold these truths to be self-evident: that all men are created equal . . . .'" His dream did not end deep down in his own heart as the assassin's bullet claimed his life in 1968. It was alive and glowing to that moment, but more important the dream stayed alive because of the millions who had the fire kindled within themselves.

Dreams will lift you to heights that have never been reached before. All people have potential. Usually, there's someone who touches your life and helps you to stretch yourself to levels that even you had not dared to dream. Maybe it has been a parent, a teacher, a coach, a businessperson, a pastor, or the author of a biography that started a fire inside you.

I can still remember reading of the great missionary pioneer who opened the continent of Africa to Christianity and to the white man, David Livingstone. He traveled over 30,000 miles on foot across that great land. By the age of ten, he was put to work in the cotton mills for up to ten hours a day. By the age of seventeen, he had paid his way through medical school. Although he had enough initiative of his own, he attributes another missionary by the name of Robert Moffat for starting a fire within his heart with these words: "I have sometimes seen in the morning sun, the smoke of a thousand villages, where no missionary has ever been." God used those words to direct Livingston to go to Africa.

Browsing through an airlines magazine, I glanced at an auto advertisement that caught my attention. It was an ad using the thought of "potential" and what that means if you have this car. In just a moment of time, I had transferred the thought about that auto into my line of work. My ministry has been with children and teens for forty years. Here's what I scribbled down:

The potential of a child often goes unrecognized, undeveloped, and unused. That's tragic. Because when the potential of a child is never developed, a terrible thing happens: *NOTHING.*

That simple little thought about the potential of an automobile, after being raised to a higher level (people), has again stirred the embers of my fire hundreds of times. I share it everywhere I go. For over twenty years now, that simple thought has helped me to *push myself!*

To each of us, that thought says go on, don't quit, don't slow down, don't let the dream fade. *Push yourself!* When I often do my little sessions of self-talk, that's one of the quotes used to remind me. Before coming to the next group of teachers to train, I will spend five to ten minutes in a back room talking to myself about the potential of those teachers in that auditorium. I'm trying to get the flames going higher so those teachers, with all their potential, will be able to see me burn from within. The goal is that they will not only hear the passion for teaching but see it in mannerisms that they too could leave fired up again!

You may do it another way, but for me self-talk so fires me up that I can't wait until the introduction is out of the way. "Turn me loose and let me burn." Self-talk is not to psyche myself up but to simply remind me of how significant the message is for those waiting to listen. You can spot the difference between genuineness and that which is artificially pumped up. May we never be there to impress our audience about us but about the dreams and ideals that lie deep within them. To do that we must *push ourselves!*

Dreams are high and lofty, but dreams will lift you to the capabilities of seeing it happen. Stay with it and find something to help *push yourself!*

It was Coca-Cola that sold only 400 Cokes in their first year of trying. Henry Ford went bankrupt twice before he founded the Ford Motor Company. Walt Disney went for months looking for a bank to loan him money to begin his theme park; in fact, 301 banks turned him down, yet he didn't give up. Disney said, "If you can dream it, you can do it. Never lose sight of the fact that this whole thing was started by a mouse." So, keep on *pushing!*

"The key today is to have both dreams and goals, passion and "ration." The starting point of any journey is a dream, a vision of some far-off possibilities. It must be exciting and moving. Once you are enthusiastic about where you are heading, then you set

some goals and bench marks that will help you to get there. When short-term goals become an end in themselves, passion fizzles out."
—Robert J. Kriegel, *If It Ain't Broke . . . Break It!*

Charles Schwab said, "When a man has put a limit on what he *will* do, he has put a limit on what he *can* do." Developing yourself to your highest abilities depends on you, not your family heritage, your disabilities, your shortage of education, or whatever. It can be changed. You may have been degraded when young, but it can end within yourself. It's about what lies within each of us. We don't have to live out our lives based on what others think or assume.

When we refuse to put the lid on our lives, we refuse to give up on life. There is still purpose, fulfillment, and achievements to be made!

Allow me here to try in a nutshell to give you the gist of a few people's lives who excelled when the odds seemed to be against them on every hand. I will try to boil their achievements down to a few sentences. Their life in book form would stir even the lazy heart to get up and try one more time. These folks refused to put the lid on their life.

Perhaps you have never read the biographies of missionaries from around the world. Here's a short sample.

Gladys Aylward

Gladys Aylward prayed, "Here's my Bible. Here's the money I have. Here is me. Find some way to use me, God!"

With that, and money enough for about two weeks, this little lady set out alone for China in 1930. Knowing only one person in China, who had died within weeks, she took over an inn and told Bible stories to the guests. China had just repealed an old and cruel practice called feet binding, which hobbled each little Chinese girl born. This practice was to keep the male in a secure state of physical superiority. Because another law said that a man could not look at a woman's foot, the Mandarin, who ran the law for the entire province, asked Gladys to inspect every house for compliance to this new law.

Now picture the only missionary in the entire province being allowed to go into every house in the land with an armed escort of soldiers and being paid to do so. And the government allowed her to make Christians of the people at her request. Later, God used her to house, clothe, and feed 200 orphans. She spoke to over 500 monks in a monastery. She worked in a leper colony. She was forced to watch over 200 believers beheaded because they would not turn from God to communism. In 1970, memorial services were held all over the world for this little lady who refused to put the lid on her life. And that's not half of the story.

Jim Elliot

In college, a speaker told Jim Elliot about the savage Auca tribe in Ecuador. Immediately his heart burned for the Quichua Indians. In Ecuador there were high mountain ranges, coastal plains, and dense jungles. In his diary he kept during college, Jim wrote, "He is no fool who gives what he cannot keep to gain what he cannot lose." He put no lid on his life.

After several flyovers of the targeted jungle location, the companion missionaries felt it was time to land. When home base received no communication from the plane, they felt it was time to investigate. A search plane spotted four bodies floating in the water. All had been killed.

Just six years later, the wives were able to reach a few for Christ. Later, most all came to know the Lord, and the savagery had ended. And it all started because some young men refused to put the lid on their lives. Within a few years, almost all had turned to Christianity.

William Booth

From the book series *Men of Faith* William Booth grew up in poverty and as a child worked as much as sixteen hours a day. He missed schooling. Booth's motto became, "Go for souls, and go for the worst."

At the age of thirty-six, with the poor on his heart, Booth started the now famous Salvation Army. He was often stoned, hit, cursed and almost killed. In one year, over 650 Salvation Army members were beaten.

By 1879, the Salvation Army had 81 stations, 127 full-time evangelists, and 7,500 services a year. In 1880, it expanded to the

United States, France, and India. In America, in 1886 Booth spoke 200 hours and was heard by 180,000 people. When he died, 40,000 people attended his funeral, including Queen Mary of England.

Booth's "Army" now included 21,203 officers and 8,972 societies in 59 countries and 34 languages around the world. When no one else would help the poor, he refused to put that lid on his life. The world is still benefitting from his work.

George Muller

Early in his ministry, George Muller refused the church salary, saying, "Forever more I will trust no one but God." Muller decided to help the street children. As he cared for these little castaways, they increased in number to forty, and the food bill increased. Again he refused to tell anyone of a need.

During his lifetime in Bristol, England, more than $7 million would be prayed in for the work. This was in the middle 1880s, and not one single person had ever been asked to give. (Wow! This is somewhat different from what we see on TV today.)

Muller listed his prayers and God's answers in a personal diary, revealed at his death. In his lifetime, 50,000 specific prayers were answered, with thousands of answers on the same day they were prayed. He said that when feeding even 2,000 orphans a day, not one meal was more than thirty minutes late.

At the end of most days, there was no money left for the next. Often money had to be prayed in before there was food for breakfast.

What a life! But Muller refused to put the lid on his goals. He *pushed himself!*

Sophie Muller

This little lady was already a gifted writer and artist in New York. She stopped briefly one afternoon when she recognized some old friends, Jack and Marge Wyrtzen, the founders of Word of Life. She stayed too long and became a Christian on that day. Within about three months, she was off to Bible school and then headed to the jungles and the headhunters in Columbia, South America. To the best of my recall, here's what this little lady accomplished.

No other missionary had ever been in that jungle. It was so far beyond civilization that it took a letter a full year and a half to return. Evangelist Jack Wyrtzen met her years later in a Miami airport. She said she had so many things wrong with her that the doctors didn't think she would ever recover, so she was heading back to the jungles. He asked her how many missionaries were down there now. "None. Just me." How many believers now? "Oh, about 12,000." How many churches? "Oh, about 240. But if we counted them as you do in America, we'd have a lot more. We don't even count them until they are baptized and have stopped their smoking, drinking, dope, and dancing."

Do you get the picture? One little lady living with headhunters had to listen day after day to learn their language. She then created their alphabet and put it down on paper to teach them. Then she taught them their language, instead of bits and pieces. Then she had to translate the Bible in tribe after tribe. No one had ever reached these people before, but that didn't put the lid on her life. When we read about such courageous lives, we should run to *push ourselves!*

Key Thoughts to Remember/Action Tips

1. This is up close and personal the older you become. But that's all right, for everyone eventually will face the lid some day.
2. The lid is sometimes pulled up a little at a time when I fail to look at my written goals for months at a time. I still have them, but I begin to justify my lack of effort.
3. Regular attention to the goal avoids the lid. How often is that for you?
4. Scheduled (on your calendar) effort on a direct step to your goal is a key!
5. Read again the brief listing of people who gave all they had for as long as they lived: Gladys Aylward, Jim Elliot, William Booth, George Muller, and Sophie Muller.

20

It Takes Self-Discipline To Push Myself!

Preview...

No one's an expert here, but we can all improve far above our present status. Self-discipline doesn't tire you out; it energizes you and give you that *push* you need.

I can't rise above average without self-discipline in place.

Self-discipline gets us striving. Through this quality we *push ourselves!*

*S*elf-discipline is the topic no one wants to talk about. I can already anticipate it hurting me somehow. I've never been good at that. I've tried that before, but it didn't last. I'm pushing myself too hard now. What's the use? I only work forty hours and go home. It's not my company; that's his problem. On and on we could go with why it's good, but not necessarily for me.

Yet, the lack of self-discipline and most of what we have already covered in this book will not be in full force, and my whole life may just be ordinary or average. I don't care for either.

In his book *An Enemy Called Average*, John L. Mason states, "Mediocrity is a region bounded on the north by compromise, on the south by indecision, on the east by past thinking, and on the west by lack of vision." That's why I don't want any of it in my life. We all fail often, and we all have our ups and downs. But I must discipline myself that it doesn't last long and doesn't happen as often as before.

Your success is up to you. You will have your deadbeats, your critics, your enemies, and your so-called friends, but they can't stop you. Everyone else who is doing something will have plenty of armchair quarterbacks screaming from the stands, just like you. It doesn't matter. You alone will either discipline yourself to be above all that or lack the discipline, which will cause you to succumb to those everyday pressures. That's being average, and I refuse to live my life as an average.

"Your potential is really up to you. It doesn't matter where you came from. It doesn't even matter what you might have believed about yourself at a previous time in your life. It's about what lies within you and whether you can bring it out".
—John Maxwell, *Talent Is Never Enough*

The stories throughout history are abundant with those who rose up from the little tiny no-name towns and backwoods roots to tackle great dreams and accomplish feats no one else would tackle. It is within you, and it can come out and take you far! Set your mind to meet those goals. Set your plan to complete those uncompleted tasks.

William James said, "Nothing is so fatiguing as the hanging on of an uncompleted task." Self-discipline doesn't tire you out; it energizes you and gives you that *push* you need.

Self-discipline is one of those characteristics we all attribute to the high achievers of our day and throughout history. We all admire it, we want it, we know it can help us or break us, yet few choose to live under such control.

Self-discipline is not our taskmaster. There are not severe stringencies we place upon ourselves to hobble or humble us, but we choose to put in place that which will always *push ourselves!* I need it. I must have it. I can't rise above average without discipline in place. When we learn the "self" part of self-discipline, we begin to take control of our lives and the production that our life can yield. Self-discipline gets us striving. Through this quality, we *push ourselves!*

In *The Miracle of Self-Discipline*, Brian Tracy states, "Persistence is your measure of your beliefs in yourself and what you are doing. The more you persist the more you believe in yourself. In reality, persistence is self-discipline in action." This is excellent advice for us all.

That habit of persistence, staying with the stuff, forging ahead, taking steps to the goal, all happened when I was disciplined enough to keep myself moving until it became my habit. It became me. It became part of my routine, or my work ethic. Discipline keeps me in line until I see the great value of the practice and the emptiness without it. Discipline has brought me to the good character practice of persistence! Wow! Self-discipline is almost like a cure-all for all my weaknesses. We all need it, and we all can have it!

Now let me try to show how self-discipline is the key to all values we have mentioned so far. We must have it. We must *push ourselves* to have a strong quality in our life called self-discipline. Look at how it ties directly into every key point of the book:

1. **Effort Proves the Stuff You Are Made Of!**
   John Wooden said, "Effort is the ultimate measure of your success."

2. **Fulfillment Keeps the Dreams Alive!**
   One of the reasons you can consistently exercise self-discipline is because the end result brings that wonderful feeling of fulfillment. You have felt it before, and you want more. That is *your push* to continue being in control of yourself.

3. **Out-achieving Myself Is the Best Comparison!**
   It will take self-discipline to out-achieve yourself. It's not always easy to break your old records. Self-discipline is your hope.

4. **The Greatest Mover—the "Mission"!**
   If you started on a worthwhile mission, that intrinsic moti-

vation (call it self-motivation) keeps the pedal to the metal as you speed toward the goal. The goal is where the significance is. Self-discipline and self-motivation are akin, with both moving steady toward the goal.

5. Influence Pushes Others Longer Than You Can Live!

It's what outlasts you. It's what will endure beyond your years. Your influence, your legacy, keeps reminding you to persist, to endure, to overcome. All of that comes through self-discipline.

6. Developing Strategy Gives Me the Green Light!

A green light is a motivational signal for self-discipline to kick in immediately. The faster you go, the easier to keep the momentum going. When my strategy tells me how to get there, just flash me a green light and my foot heads for the gas pedal!

7. Decisiveness Gets Me off the Dime!

Again, self-discipline is a key here. Getting yourself moving always takes self-discipline. It moves us out of lethargy, laziness, and whatever is holding us back. Take stock. Am I moving or am I at anchor? Are my sails set for the mighty winds that can move my vessel, my crew, and my cargo to any destination I desire? I must discipline myself.

8. Evaluation Initiates Greater Achievements!

Many in leadership roles still fail to evaluate their successes and failures. Self-discipline must kick in with a strong push to learn from evaluations how to improve our position from adequate to excellent. Evaluation is too significant to ignore or delay.

9. Focus Keeps Me on Target!

Without self-discipline, focus will not automatically keep you on track. It is the discipline that keeps you focused. Without it, we all have the tendency to look away from the main goal more than we used to. Remember the old saying, "Out of sight, out of mind."

10. Innovation Will Solve My Problems, Pushing Me Forward!

If I am not self-disciplined enough to think my way through my problems, my problems never seem to go away. Innovation takes time, and self-discipline forces you to take that time.

11. The Team Will Take Me There!

No person will last long as a one-man show when a team is needed. When you know the project is above and beyond the Lone Ranger's ability, self-discipline must push you to build your team.

12. Vision Keeps My Dream in Sight!

Vision sees the dream. Strategy plans the steps to the dream. Self-discipline keeps you on track.

13. Using Time Wisely Stretches My Days!

If there is ever an area that helps you to use time wisely, it's the discipline of yourself. Time is all I have. Self-discipline will *push me* to get the most out of it.

14. Increased Passion Moves Me!

Passion will focus you on the goal that brings you the most fulfillment. The trait of self-discipline will ensure I am always fulfilled.

15. Reading Inspires Me, Motivates Me, and Pushes Me!

Again, apart from self-discipline, the daily habit of reading will never get started or will decline rapidly. Not creative? Read from a creative writer and use his techniques—now you're creative! Your personal creativity will be greatly enhanced by feeding your mind as much as possible. Take someone else's idea and tweak it a bit to meet your needs.

You are being creative! Now, discipline yourself to read, and you're on your way.

16. Clarifying My Role Settles My To-Do List!

Most of us would rather assume our people know exactly what's on our minds rather than take the time to carefully and fully explain what is. Apart from discipline applied to myself, it may be left up to my team or my employees to assume what they can't see in my mind. Clear the air. Explain your goal carefully because the team is who will take you there. Exercise self-discipline, the personal *pushing* of yourself.

17. Faith Is Your Supernatural Push!

We examine (a) Faith for eternal life, (b) Faith for living, and (c) Faith for wisdom, knowledge, and understanding. We need it all for today, tomorrow, and throughout life.

18. Goals Push Me Out of My Comfort Zone!

Aha! This is another area that demands self-discipline. When goals are weak or absent, where's the *push*? The leader must see the value of goals for himself and for his workforce. Goals get you striving toward that mark! Achievement is motivated by goals. Excitement and momentum grow as goals come nearer. Discipline moves me out of my comfort zone.

19. Refusing to Put the Lid On Pushes Me above Ordinary!

Finally, self-discipline keeps me driving, pursuing, and striving, which in turn keeps the lid off. The sky's the limit. The horizon always leads to more. The world doesn't stop where the sky meets the ocean. As Columbus believed, from here to there is only the first big step. When I discipline myself, I can keep the dream alive and in sight!

20. It Takes Self-Discipline to Push Yourself!

There it is—there's *your push!* It will make you or break you in all of these areas. I choose to discipline myself. I choose to dream greater dreams. I choose to set my steps (goals) in order to take one more step closer. I'm sure that's what you want. *Push yourself!*

The musician doesn't begin at the top, but discipline will get her there!
The laborer disciplines himself to the workload or he is fired!
The teacher will not improve unless he disciplines himself!
The preacher will improve when time to study improves!
The mechanic could improve training, if he would try!
The NBA and NFL players must have self-discipline, plus whatever the coaches can add in training! Their off-season must still require self-discipline or they may lose their spot on the team when they return out of shape.
The housewife will ignore dirt and organization without self-discipline!

There is only one exception I have found: Barney Fife never ever improved.

Conclusion

So, what do we learn from all of this? We must learn the significance of self-discipline. It is sometimes hard to learn, hard to retain, and hard to maintain. However, it is this very discipline that will take us above and beyond our wildest dreams and the dreams we have yet to dream. It will make us achievers all our lives. It will make our work so desirous that we plan to get another hour out of every day by rising earlier. We will take hold of our schedules. We will do those top 20 percent projects that are more significant than the other 80 percent. We will use the twenty values from our study to aid every area of our careers. *Push yourself* to make it so!

CPSIA information can be obtained at www.ICGtesting.com
Printed in the USA
BVOW03s0053280314

349006BV00005B/10/P